BEHOLD THE MAN

THE MACMILLAN COMPANY
NEW YORK · BOSTON · CHICAGO · DALLAS
ATLANTA · SAN FRANCISCO

MACMILLAN & CO., Limited
LONDON · BOMBAY · CALCUTTA
MELBOURNE

THE MACMILLAN COMPANY
OF CANADA, Limited
TORONTO

BEHOLD THE MAN

A Picture in Four Aspects

BY

FRIEDRICH RITTELMEYER, PH.D.

Authorized Translation by
ERICH HOFACKER
and
GEORGE BENNETT HATFIELD

According to the
Second Edition, 1920

THE MACMILLAN COMPANY
1929

NEW YORK

Copyright, 1929,
By THE MACMILLAN COMPANY.

Set up and electrotyped.

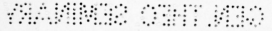

PREFATORY NOTICE TO THE FIRST
EDITION, 1912

THIS little book shows on the face its origin in four lectures. And this setting is, we hope, a fortunate one, especially for assembling a total effect in a clear, simple form. For the sake of securing a likeness of the inner nature of Jesus, it has been thought best to omit entirely the material and apparatus of scientific scholarship, and, in the end, even the references themselves. He who wishes to become acquainted with the purely scientific work which has been done on the Gospels may acquire the historical fundamentals from the little book: *Urevangelium: Jesus der Christ, Bericht und Botschaft in erster Gestalt,* (The Original Gospel: Jesus Christ, Account and Message in Its First Form), by Resa.

Since there is no scarcity of such books as give the things which are historically known about Jesus, we hope that it will prove a welcome change to many a reader to receive this invitation to join the author in an effort to reëxperience the eternal values which are found even in the historically approved facts regarding the life of Jesus. It needs mention expressly, however, that the picture of Jesus which is drawn here is proof against any loss of worth because of the results of historical investigation.

Any innermost impression whatsoever, though it

might be examined conscientiously again and again, will always turn out to be something personal and something for which words are entirely inadequate. Therefore, the request can fairly be made that the reader will earnestly try to use his innermost sympathy in recreating the complete picture for himself. For the superficial reader who asks only for something new and who does not know how to penetrate through the words to that which is clearly inexpressible, these lectures are not intended.

Someone has said that our time suffers from weariness over an excess of discussion about Jesus. For those who suffer from these trying discussions and from the strife which goes on even over whether Christ was a myth, this little book will bring, we hope, at least some small relief. That it may reach as far as possible all those to whom it has something to give is the heartiest wish of its author.

FRIEDRICH RITTELMEYER

TRANSLATORS' PREFACE

THE translators have been led to offer an English translation of this book by a conviction that it will unquestionably prove to be of value and interest to American readers. The author, Dr. Rittelmeyer, is one of the foremost religious leaders in Central Europe to-day. He is known for his critical studies of Nietzsche, for his work as editor of religious journals, for the excellency of his preaching when a minister in Nuremberg and in Berlin, and for a number of books, all of them marked by delicacy of feeling and force of expression.

Dr. Rittelmeyer has told elsewhere how he planned, when a very young man, to write a book on Jesus. To this task he afterwards gave about twenty years. To this end he studied first the strongest opponents of Jesus, such as Nietzsche; then the great rivals of Jesus, such as Buddha; then the great followers of Jesus, such as St. Francis, Meister Eckhart, and Tolstoi. This plan he followed, he says, in order to be able better to present a full portrait of Jesus, and one which would at the same time be the result of his own impressions and evaluations. He aims to draw what he calls a "total picture," by which he means not an assemblage of various historical conclusions put together in a mosaic, but a picture of Jesus that his readers will agree depicts and defines

7

an organic unity. Jesus has been studied by many other men from single, personal angles during the centuries. Dr. Rittelmeyer seeks to make the full round of the circle and then to convey the "total effect" produced upon his mind and heart. The reader will note readily how that purpose regulates the form of his exposition.

The translators have endeavored with all patience to give a faithful translation, and at the same time to preserve the personal touch of the author.

THE TRANSLATORS

University of Pittsburgh
December, 1928

CONTENTS

PART I
THE LIFE

BEHOLD THE MAN

PART I

THE LIFE

The breath of a great time touches us still when we read what the Gospels relate to us of John the Baptist. Only a few faint sounds and broken snatches out of his full speech come down to us across the centuries. "And think not to say within yourselves, We have Abraham to our father: for I say unto you, that God is able of these stones to raise up children unto Abraham." As he said these words, *abanim banim,* he might have taken up a stone lying by the wayside and held it up before their eyes. So stood he before them a compact embodiment of trust in God, a pulsing spirit of independence toward men and opinions. "Whose fan is in his hand, and he will thoroughly purge his floor, and gather his wheat into the garner; but he will burn up the chaff with unquenchable fire." "And now also the axe is laid to the root of the tree: therefore, every tree which bringeth not forth good fruit is hewn down and cast into the fire." "I indeed baptize you with water unto repentance: but he that cometh after me is mightier than I, whose shoes I am not worthy to bear: he shall baptize you with the Holy Ghost and with fire."

13

Only a few words, but they suffice to give John
place among the first preachers of all times and
enroll him among the greatest of the prophets.
few bits of ruins in an open field can betray the great
spirit who once built there. And so these few words
reveal a preacher of impressive weight and popu-
larity. They show him to be a man of austere and
significant greatness, a prophet free from all selfish
expectations and aflame with the fire of God. Here
speaks a kind of manhood scarcely found in our own
age, grown as the trees of his own desert grew, storm-
tested, gnarled, and hardened like steel. His figure
towers over its surroundings like the rocks of the
wasteland, lonely and inexorable. But this man is,
in truth, humanly great, and he is great above all in
this—that although himself an austere ascetic, he
asks of others no superhuman efforts, but instead
plays a light divine upon those duties that are
nearest and most pressing. "Exact no more than
that which is appointed to you." "Soldiers, do
violence to no man, neither accuse any falsely; and
be content with your wages." Nothing more does
God demand from you! Such is the simple and
clear humanity which, like a beautiful laurel crown,
adorns the head of this man who is himself rugged
and grown hard like steel.

John's period of activity could not have lasted
long, but he worked with prodigious power. Here
was preaching as it ought to be, the kind that breaks
forth from a man as from a volcano. A volcano
speaks when the deeps below can contain themselves
no longer; it can do nothing of itself. Silent it has

, stand until its molten heart gets ready to move,
limb to its brim and break forth out of bounds to
lluminate and to overflow the countryside far and
wide. It was like that with John. And the belching
of his anger when it burst was like the lurid light of
bursting lava, which awakens the sleepy from their
lethargy. That fire threw its light across the land
until its lengthening radius reached a distant
village, where an unknown man recognized the signal
as ⅃ 's call and came forth to enter upon the great
mission of His life.

What Jesus experienced at the Jordan and in
the Wilderness of Judea is pictured for us as in the
etching of a cloud on the vault of heaven, in the
sweeping outlines of His visions; and its significance
is conveyed to us with all the concise matter-of-
factness of an ancient cuneiform tablet. Then and
there the certainty laid hold of Him vehemently
that He had been chosen for extraordinary things.
Then and there took place the first decisive engage-
ment, sharply defined, momentous, inescapable—a
struggle between the call of His insight of God upon
His allegiance and the expectations of His people.
Incomparably sublime experiences thronged a human
soul in that hour. He perceived himself seized of
God directly: "Thou art my beloved Son, whom I
have chosen." Unconditionally and without hesitation, whole-heartedly and keeping nothing back, He,
in turn, laid hold of God. He undertook to trust in
God alone, to ask nothing for Himself, never to act
on His own initiative, but always and everywhere to
serve God alone.

No valid reason can be cited why we should mi.
trust that which the story of the Baptism and th
story of the Temptation relate. But there is abun-
dant reason why we should be gripped by the greatness of His experiences and meet their demands upon
our reverence. And the terse, matter-of-fact account
which the Gospels give of His seizure by God con-
veys to a sensitive spirit infinitely more than it can
find in the attempt of a modern poet like Frenssen
to recreate the atmosphere of these events; after all,
such poetic efforts in no way do justice to the magni-
tudes of the inner life of the ancient peoples.

Not long after these events Jesus found Himself
in a situation which virtually compelled Him to
enter upon a dramatic, startling course of public
activity. He began, however, in the simplest and
most natural way, by taking advantage of the oppor-
tunity to speak at the close of the regular service of
worship in the synagogue. As to the impression His
words made, the record contains a highly important
statement. "For this man speaks as one having
authority, and not as the scribes." In these words
we feel even to-day the note of reality that tells of
an unusual impression. Wholly different from the
overscrupulous rabbis, with their display of learning
and their narrow spirit, was the free, bold speech of
Jesus. As we would express it in the language of
to-day: This was not one more spell of mere speech
"about" God; it was the novelty of a God presence
within determined to find outlet in speech. It was
no such form of speech as uses words to delight the
ear and please the mind; it was the vehicle of a

wer which penetrated into the very life of the
arer. It was no mere talking; it was action,
pressive and effective. And it was not the deed
f the man who spoke, but the deed of the Higher
One who empowered Him to exercise a persuasive
influence upon the world.

On hearing the words of Jesus even to-day, our
own response is closely akin to that of the unknown
author who first felt and told us his impression.
Words like the following come to us with all the
driving force of a storm from above, capable of carrying the hearts of men by their power straight toward
the Kingdom of God: "No man having put his hand
to the plow and looking back, is fit for the Kingdom
of God." "And if thy right eye offend thee, pluck
it out, and cast it from thee." "Follow me; and let
the dead bury their dead." "And for the joy thereof
he goeth and selleth all that he hath, and buyeth
that field." This is the stride that is native to the
man with mind made up who never comes to a halt.
This is a martial call sounded by the man who is
deterred by no conditions, whom no obstacles can
stop. This is the great hour of the world's Conqueror, and His clarion words sweep with the head-
long force of a storm over the earth. The passage-
way into a new and higher world with a hidden glory
at its heart is now to be thrown open. Prostrate
under His feet lies the old world as He pushes resist-
lessly straight ahead through this passage into the
Kingdom of God. Already a breath is ours of free,
pure air from the mountain peaks of a holier world.

Nothing has any value left, no value whatever

compared to the value of the One Great Thing th
is to come. The world and the worldly life sir
from sight before this mighty mystery. The Spir:
in sublime freedom and in dauntless power lays hol
of His new Kingdom. Everything is changed from
within as if by miraculous power. The speech of
commission which Jesus delivered to His disciples
lets us more fully and with greater clearness than
any other words of His into the secret of just how
He Himself felt at that time. Out of the tropics of
of these words blows a Power bringing as it were a
springtime of God, matchless in beauty and able to
make all things new. With the one inclusive divine
message, "The Kingdom of God is here!" were th
disciples to wander through the Kingdoms of this
world. While they are to be superior to circumstances and not dependent on human assistance, yet
they are to be willing to accept with modesty whatever is offered gladly to them. They are not to live
a life beset by needs, and in spending themselves
are to do so on a gloriously unheeding, unbounded,
inexhaustible scale. Joyous but not self-exultant in
the hour of victory, nor dazzled by its glory, they
shall remain steadfast in allegiance to the one great
task of serving as the voice of God, first to call and
then to win the world, because their being is wholly
transformed.

In this one great major chord, whoso will may
hear the innermost tones of the feel which life possessed for the heart of Jesus. Here he may come
close enough to life to hear His soul breathe. In this
key, He felt freest. He spoke most freely, and

He acted most freely in that first uniquely glorious springtime.

The impact of the miracles of Jesus, however, made a stronger impression than His words upon His contemporaries. Miracles!—a word foreign to our minds to-day. Many a person who would like to walk about in the Garden of the Gospels, enjoying this word and that word, which are so like divine flowers in bloom, are struck with distaste by the presence therein of these strange, foreign growths—the stories of miracles; and too often such a person turns away and seldom revisits the Garden. 'ut let us look into the calyx of these exotic flowers. Closer examination will, perhaps, show that they)elong to the narrative. We could, to be sure, dispense to-day with the accounts of these miracles. If increasing knowledge should compel us to accept the view that all of them without exception arose through the lack of skill in understanding the processes of nature, or through turning fable into fact in the case of some of the parables, or that they came about through the methods by which folklore builds its myths, we might, indeed, even then believe that in rejecting them we would suffer no religious loss. But just because our minds have, to-day, become clearer and calmer as to the significance of these accounts and the nature of ancient miracles, we are able to discern the elements of reality which lie back of these alleged deeds of Jesus. Is it not true that these records contain features of the nature of proof of the historical foundations of these events?

As we, to-day, read many of these wonder stories

with all their vivid details—such as the cure of the
man with the palsy who is let down through the
roof, or the account of the conversation with the
Syro-Phoenician mother over the crumbs given even
to the dogs—we cannot refrain from imagining how
these stories would probably sound if they had been
simply invented; nor can we refrain from making
a comparison between them and other stories which
obviously are invented tales, like some of those
about Mohammed, or the stories concerning Jesus
in the later legendary gospels. As we do this, many
a notable remark that is worthy of credence on its
own merit will attract our attention. Recall, fo
instance, the admission of Jesus that he was not abl
to do any miracle in Nazareth, and perceive how in
His bold, free use of a Scripture reference He
explained His situation and offered His defense.
Again, in His earnest altercation with the Pharisees who seek to reproach Him by saying that He
does His works in the name of Satan, we note that
His answer is couched in this same popularly graphic
style, in energetic words that are surcharged with
a note of finality. We think of His words of sorrow
over the cities which are mentioned as the scenes
where most of His works were done and are forced
to ask, Do they not presuppose that those works
really occurred? The description of His concern
and the precautions which He took lest the people
should think of Him chiefly as a worker of magic
is all the more convincing for its unobtrusiveness.
When we give our attention exclusively to Jesus
Himself, we see how much alive, how humanly near

and great appears His ardent insistence that the
purity of His works must be guarded, and that no
taint of personal reward must be permitted to cast
any reflection upon His true, inner motive—the
highest good for men. If we group all such characteristics of these accounts together we believe they
cannot readily be explained as due merely to the
invention, or even to the bias of later writers and
biographers. The only explanation which is ten-
able must look upon them as chapters of the living
experience of Jesus Himself and of His immediate
associates.

Much of this body of material still remains hope-
lessly opaque and inscrutable. But to set out with
a light heart to tear up by the roots these accounts
of miracles in the Garden of the Gospels, instead
of treating this whole field of material with careful
discrimination—this is for us, now, after all, an
impossible course. The Scriptural records can be
so construed as to lead us, we feel sure, to a closer
approximation to the reality of things as it was
experienced by the hearts of men in those days
than we should find in this complete rejection. We
calmly wait with patience and sympathy for the
discovery of the key to all these conditions, and we
may well hope that the features in the narrative
which we do not now understand will one day be
explained in all their particulars. Some day, we
believe, not only will the genesis of these narratives
become clear, but we shall also truly understand the
thoughts of the men who recorded them. Even the
next few decades may bring to us proof sufficient to

show that our much-praised sense of what constitutes reality has been blind to innumerable bits of reality, important bits which more primitive Christians perceived and firmly grasped. Around the figure of Jesus strange lights played and extraordinary things happened. Through all the accounts which have come down to us, one supreme fact stands out clearly: instead of having broken natural laws, the probability is that forces operating by natural laws other than those familiar to us broke out into action through Him, natural laws of a higher kind, that is, accessible to, and indigenous in such a lofty nature as was His, but unknown to our present ignorance. We do not think rightly if we think of His acts as external signs in token of a power which God bestowed upon Him—as one person might show to another a badge of authorization. We interpret truly when we understand that the signs He gave were witnesses from within, from the work of God within Him, and that these signs are to be regarded as a revelation of their Source, just as the rays which radiate from the sun reveal its inmost nature.

Let all this be as it may. Those who have felt dissatisfaction with the Gospel writers for relating so many accounts of miracles in place of more copious citations of the words of Jesus, which nearly all readers of the Gospels have longed for, will one day be grateful as they perceive that precisely in this respect these ancient recorders have been deeply loyal and faithful to the uniqueness of the life of Jesus. For the life of Jesus was, above all things

else, an epic succession of deed, conflict, and conquest. Well He knew that distress serves as an
oper door to blessedness. His life was to Him, as
those who give us the record of His life realized, an
intensely personal war against the power of evil.
The thought-forms and the world-ideas of Jesus
are unquestionably in some instances, it is true, foreign to the modern mind. Nevertheless, the sublime
mood of 's Man who felt Himself so placed in
direct p 1 opposition to Satan that the living
out of H 1became a dramatic interpretation of
hat opp (grips the mind of our time, or of any
time, all nore powerfully. He believed, it has
already b said, in the realm of demonic spirits.
That is tr But how evident it is that He never
permitted e cruder extremes of that belief to
obtrude th nselves; yea, rather, with what energy
did He kee j them in the background!

In what a thoroughly human light does He place,
and with what perfect insight does he detect, every
form of human distress and confer upon it His own
holy spirit! How buoyantly does He live, full of
light and freedom, sustained by the certainty that
nothing evil any longer has power—is powerless
indeed, for all time to come. How royal is His
bearing due to His feeling of victory over all the
sinister forces of darkness around Him! He appears
triumphantly great just for this reason: that in the
full splendor of a conqueror He does not draw back
from personal encounter with the power of evil at
its highest tide. Even unto the last days of His
life, when He withdrew into Himself that in silence

He might hold on to the end, His very non-resistance produced the peculiar effect of a well-chosen attack upon His enemies before they could make their assault. The coming of a conqueror into the world with a symphony of qualities and powers which render Him sure that all fearsome things, human or superhuman, have forever lost their fearsomeness, and the overcoming by this conqueror of all that is hardest and all that is darkest through the power of His unquenchable consciousness of victory—that is the story of Jesus.

Upon every act of Jesus that we know lies the stamp of nobility and of highest manliness. The time will soon come, we believe, when those who are real men will know no joy more stimulating than that of simply looking upon Him. Whether He chances to be active or passive when we are looking, the stimulus He exerts is perpetually positive, and to know Him thus is a perennial joy, a good that does not diminish if our contemplation be prolonged.

Some such ideal as that—an ideal entirely different from that which the earlier followers of Jesus cherished—will in our judgment yet fill and conquer the earth. What ground is there for this statement? It is obvious from the record that His radiant vitality and deep joy, itself truly active even while He was passive, could not blind Jesus to the truth that His work would be misinterpreted unless it were buttressed by His forcefully spoken word. There is a simple incident which brings to us a clear glimpse of the deep inner struggle going on in the

mind of Jesus. One morning, after a day of exceptionally vigorous activity, Jesus was nowhere to be
found by His disciples. He had taken refuge in the
holiness of isolation, in the sanctuary of solitude,
that He might there listen to the voice of God and
obtain personal replenishment. When the disciples
seek Him and at last He is discovered in His holy
hiding place, He announces to their astonishment
that henceforth He will subordinate the much-
ught and highly praised activity of healing in
or of the unostentatious and thankless task of
aching. And so Jesus began to teach—sometimes
the synagogue, sometimes by the lake; now on
he mountainside, now in the homes He visited.
Sometimes great throngs heard Him, while again He
was attended only by the small circle of disciples;
sometimes the teaching was given in short, aphoris-
tic sayings, and again in full-length parables. Exceedingly simple as it was, it was the most epoch-
making teaching ever done in human history. It
was even monotonous in its methodical perseverance, though at the most it went on for barely three
years, and perhaps for no more than a year or a few
months.

But soon the field of struggle was changed for
Him and another problem became His primary concern. As we see Him at first, His whole soul had
urged Him on into a mighty crusade against the
tragic misery of man in all its varying forms. But
now a wholly different kind of conflict was forced
upon Him: the strife with friends as well as with
foes—friends who were unconsciously His enemies,

and enemies who in truth ought to have been His friends.

Jesus had now continually to defend Himself against His friends. The very persons who adored Him would in their unwise enthusiasm divert His work into false paths. He was also compelled to turn against the leaders of the people because their hostility threatened to annul His aims and His plans. The struggle Jesus waged here against His opponents in order to preserve His aims reveal when it is considered in its entirety, a dominati and persuasive force that is unique in the history religious convictions. He, a solitary individual, con fronts them in their collective power. A lone com batant, He proceeds to challenge their combined authority. Single-handed He is able to cope with their every charge, able to meet every weapon in their armory, be it intelligence, spirit, ability, or executive power. Even in those instances where his opponents took the initiative against Him with all their craft and malice, He was able almost in an instant when it came His turn to throw them back upon the defensive. He is ever the solitary protagonist of His cause, and the thought never seems to occur to His disciples that they might help Him. He always pushes straight ahead with undeviating perseverance, no matter what the conditions or sons for yielding. He feels no fear and do His full freedom; He is incapable of retre and never resorts to the use of duplicity. An attack from any quarter puts His whole cause into jeopardy for Him, but He never allows Himself to be drawn into

controversy over side issues. He soon brings the
basic issue to the front and compels decision with an
insistence that challenges the very soul of His
assailant. It must be remembered that He belonged
to a people who lived and moved under the shadow
of religious authority, a people who in all matters,
great and small, even to the most insignificant,
depended for guidance completely upon their
learned men; a people, moreover, who had accu-
ulated a vast store of traditional piety by their
evotion to these leaders. For Jesus to assert Him-
elf so freely in the midst of such a people and to
roclaim His unpalatable message so unqualifiedly
the face of this whole body of constituted author-
signifies evidence, we believe, of dimensions
most beyond the range of our powers of apprecia-
. The ancient prophets of Israel, it is true, had
pled single-handed with the tyranny of a tradi-
and had grown stereotyped. But Jesus waged
ecisive war of all time against this form of
us. ation. The unforced self-assurance, the calm
certainty, and the atmosphere of sovereignty which
He brought to this great act of emancipation give
rise to an unending wonder and delight which never
seem to go deep enough. Never has a crusade for
so priceless a stake been entered upon with a purer
purpose by a crusader freer from sinking spells of
discouragement.

Close insight into the clash of ideals between
Jesus and His enemies is obtainable from the narratives of His encounters with them, notwithstand-
ing that so much time has intervened. Their ina-

bility to understand why He would heal on the
Sabbath is a searchlight that helps explain the situation from many angles. Here is testimony that is
testimony indeed to the strength and superiority of
His own insight over blind tradition in the fact that
He would not observe the ingrained oriental habit
of resting on the Sabbath. His change of the day
of rest into a day of love bears witness to a life which
was always true to its own nature and which chose
its course in response to the inner necessity of it
being.

There is here, too, it may be noted, obvious ind.
rect proof of the reality of His extraordinary acts
of healing. For the chief interest of the writers of
the Gospels is not in these deeds themselves but in
the time of their occurrence. We feel here all the
more by contrast how inflexible and rigid was that
customary piety which could cause a man, instead
of rejoicing, to protest with indignation that a sufferer had been healed on the Holy Sabbath. How
could they dare to show indignation? Precisely
because customary opinion held that a peculiar relation existed between the observance of the Sabbath
and the hopes of tragic Israel. For if only a single
Sabbath—so they taught in town and village—were
to be perfectly observed by the people, then the
Kingdom of God would surely come; it could not
then be far off. For such an inviolate Sabbath God
had waited, and still would wait.

But now, here is a man who on his own account
is proclaiming that the Kingdom of God, the holy
reign of God on earth, is near, and yet Himself is the

first to bring into disrepute the greatest command of
God—the command that the Sabbath be kept inviolate. This man who professes to be sent from God
Himself shows open contempt for the Sabbath of
God instead of observing its holiness more strictly
and inculcating its observance even more zealously
than anybody else. How can He be the Promised
One! We hear Him say: "The Sabbath was made
or man, and not man for the Sabbath: Therefore the
 of Man is Lord also of the Sabbath." Remem-
 these words were addressed to men who ear-
tly debated among themselves whether on the
bbath a sandal should be tied with a bow or a
ot! Here we can take the pulse of the conflict
d measure its intensity and at the same time feel
e nobleness of the life of unaggressive nonconform-
ty which was thus lived. A wonderful, compelling
note of pure fidelity to humanity sounds through all
the din raised by this legalism, which in those days
confused men and held them in thrall.

We understand even more clearly the temper of
the opposition to Jesus when we note that other
reproach which the Jewish leaders cast at Him: "This
man does not turn his back upon sinners, but even
eats with them!" It is difficult for us to realize
to-day the tempest of anger which Jesus aroused in
these men by any kindly gesture of fellowship
toward outcasts—publicans and harlots they were,
scoundrels and prostitutes! What sort of scandal-
ous saint must He be to make companions of such
people! The wrath of all the good and righteous
spent itself upon these creatures. Were they not,

indeed, the incorrigibles who by their unrepentant
sinning were forever impeding and retarding the
coming of the Kingdom of God. If only for a single twenty-four hours these dregs of society could
be swept from their midst and God's holy people be
well rid of them, then the inauguration of the Kingdom would already have taken place and all the
present unspeakable misery of the faithful children
of God would at once be at an end. What else coul
the strict servants of the law, those who out
loyalty to God had so conscientiously vexed and
mented themselves in what they thought to be
service, think of conduct like this? What a sit
tion, to be told that the Kingdom of God is at ha
and then have the bearer of the good news sit dow
at the same table with the accursed enemies of God
This forces them as earnest devotees of the law to
stand aside, while He, who says He is sent of God,
by the act of sitting down at meat with the despisers
of God, in symbolic fashion elevates them from the
status of outcasts to the position of friends to be
treated with respect and as eligible for membership
in the approaching Kingdom of God. If in our
streets to-day a prominent banker or a famous general were suddenly to appear walking with bared
head between two shorn convicts whom he calls his
brothers, the sensation that would run through the
crowd could hardly be as great.

"They that are whole have no need of a physi-
cian, but they that are sick." To us, this saying of
Jesus appears natural, humane, self-evident. In
His day, however, despite many similar sayings of

the Hebrew prophets, its truth was not received as a revelation, but it was even felt to show an erroneous and unpardonable attitude. Every man was then judged wholly according to his acts. That a person was entitled to rank and standing because his innermost nature, or his yearning desire, or his own unconscious needs, rendered him thus deserving, was a point of view that was entirely incomprehensible, a height that was completely beyond the reach of the people. But for us to-day, nothing the Gospels so moves our hearts as the attitude Jesus toward the fallen. His freedom from every conceivable prejudice in meeting sinful people could not have been more complete. Wholly unaffected by the malicious glances of the righteous, He moves with perfect ease among the outcasts and cheerfully and freely sits with them at table, and no expression of hostility can in the least disturb the quiet, unfettered joy which He takes in their utter freedom from self-satisfaction.

On the other hand, there is in His behavior toward friend or foe no suggestion either of ostentation or of opposition. Whenever a soul begins to move in the direction of the divine, we see his whole nature overflow in joy and love. In such a moment, both His words and deeds express the most heartfelt welcome, unimpeachable good will, tenderest consideration, transparent honesty, and warmest kindness. No one should fail to go behind these words and deeds of Jesus lest he miss the note of elation that resounds in them all—in the story of Zaccheus, of Mary Magdalene, of the Prodigal Son, and in the

other parables. One instinctively recalls that word
of Jesus about the joy there is in heaven over one
sinner who repents. We seem to hear a heavenly
pean sounding through them, and nowhere do we so
keenly sense that the divine itself is brought into
such close contact with our humanity in the soul of
Jesus as we do in His dealings with sinners. His
unwavering and tireles efforts to seek and save the
lost, His unconquerable love, have made men think
of Him from that time onward as a manifestation
of the innermost soul of God Himself. Like the
clarion voice of a bell floating above a confused
babel of noise, the wonder of His love speaks so as
to be heard above the din of all the sins and aber-
rations of the world.

Then, as now, it was particularly people belonging to the lowest depths of life who seemed to realize that something extraordinary was happening.
Wherever Jesus went something awoke in their
hearts and went out to meet halfway the dayspring
from on high visiting their night. When else have
human hearts been so deeply moved as we see them
in the stories of Zaccheus and of the great sinner,
Mary Magdalene?

In striking contrast, and yet a perfect comple-
ment to all the tenderness of His invitations to the
lowly, is the inflexible front with which Jesus met
the onslaughts of the religious teachers and leaders
of the people. The weapons which he used to
checkmate them were a mind dazzlingly clear and
a force of character effortlessly unyielding, more
uncompromising, indeed, than even that of John the

Baptist. The whole weight of His influence was
directed against the continued ascendancy of the
way of life championed by the traditional teachers.
He knew that liberation for His people was impossible unless He could succeed in destroying its sway.
In this He failed. For the people, in their anxiety
to observe the rules prescribed, were too much intim-
idated and enslaved by their training, too strongly
fettered and hidebound in their attachment to cus-
tom, good and bad, to be able to follow in the foot-
steps of Him whom they should have made their
leader when He appeared. They may have listened
to Him spellbound, as people listen in a dream, when
He spoke to them of life in the glorious Kingdom
of God's rule, but only to turn and sink back again
dull and listless into their imprisonment. And so it
became increasingly clear that those who clung to
tradition would ultimately triumph over the lone
leader and His new way of life.

From this time onward the thought of suffering
rose more and more prominently above the horizon
of His life. It is strange that anyone at any time
should have so misunderstood Jesus as to believe
that He did not know and foretell His suffering, or
think that He was taken unaware when it came to
Him. How exceptionally blind Jesus would have
been had He not seen the dark clouds which had
begun to loom. It is in those words of Jesus which
refer to human suffering that we sense especially
the heart of a man who feels pain keenly and who
speaks about it in terms of personal experience.
How piercingly real are His words of anticipation

concerning the cup of sorrow which He must drink and the Baptism of agony which He must receive! The sensitive reader will recognize that precisely those passages in the Gospels which record the thoughts of Jesus on suffering are the ones that bring us into closest contact with His own living reality.

The fate of John the Baptist seems to have awakened in Jesus for the first time a presentiment of His approaching suffering: "Elias has already come, and they have done with him as they would." In this remark to His disciples we still feel the august impression which the death of John the Baptist made upon his contemporaries. More especially, this event was destined to bring about in Jesus an inner struggle over the meaning of suffering and to point the way to what proved to be His deepest thoughts about God. That event also would outline in His soul an image of a Redeemer willing to suffer, and would implant its lesson so deeply in His sensitive nature that it would ere long spring into full life in His Passion.

Deep and wide extend the vistas that open before us here into the mysteries of Divine Providence. "Not the things that be of men, but the things that be of God"—in these simple words Jesus, at a later time, poignantly expressed to His disciples the fruits of a deep, inner conflict. In those words we can still feel the tenseness of the struggle, as well as the sense of victory which He, still trembling from the anguish, has now attained. It is not often that we come in the Gospels so near to the heart of Jesus as we do here. It is quite evident that Jesus did not

live His life from the beginning in the consciousness
that all His days were to be but a preparation for
great suffering at its close. But the necessity of a
via dolorosa became increasingly clear and distinct,
and more and more did He realize that the nature
of suffering is divine. He did not foresee every step
on the way to His Passion. He went up with calm
resolution to meet a future that was enveloped in
darkness. Up to the last, Jesus seems to have
remained in a state of uncertainty as to whether the
most fearful of these sufferings might not be spared
Him. The world now knows that He was strong
enough to meet the final agonies in the power of
His limitless and unshaken trust in God.

But if we mistake not, we can look yet deeper
into His gradual realization of the meaning of suffering. We note the metaphors in which He spoke: a
cup which I must drink; a baptism which I must
receive; a ransom which I must pay. Do we not
seem in touch here with a gradual ascent of His
thoughts, devoted wholly to God as they were, a
wonderful inner clarification in process? A cup
which I must drink to remain unquestionably obedient to the Father! This is the first step in His
renunciation of any further attempt to understand
the mystery of suffering. A baptism which I must
receive in order to be anointed and crowned King
of this world! This is a sign that comprehension is
at the dawn that suffering is to confer a royal dignity upon His own life. A ransom which I must
pay in order to deliver man from his bondage! This
is an indication that the understanding has at length

been made perfect to Him of God's plan to bring salvation to a world that lives in sorrow and in sin.

Have we said more about His growth in the understanding of suffering than can be strictly justified by the evidence of the records themselves? All the more firmly established, in that case, is the confidence of Jesus in God and in Himself. Even while the darkness is greatest His faith in God, the Kingdom of God, and the message of God, does not falter for a moment. His own deep-seated confidence seeks to penetrate and to illuminate even that which presents the most sinister and the most fearful appearance. At the same moment that Jesus perceived His suffering to be inevitable, the cause and reason of it became clear to Him. It could now mean nothing else than the method which God deemed indispensable to the fulfillment of His divine plan.

Never was the approach of suffering more clearly perceived by any mind nor its pain more unselfishly conquered by any heart; never was anguish more humanly experienced nor more divinely overcome than in the life of Jesus.

Before the final storm broke there came a moment of calm. In pilgrimages to the borders of the land, Jesus concealed Himself both from His unrelenting enemies as well as from uncomprehending friends. In the small circle of the most faithful and sympathetic He sought to bring about that which was now, in view of the approaching end, so highly imperative—a comprehension of His inner thoughts. Then, suddenly, if we may believe the records, a passionate restlessness seizes Him, and to the dismay of these faithful ones He sets His face directly toward Jerusalem. To Jerusalem he pressed unswervingly, keeping well in the lead of His disciples, now as if He were bent on an encounter with His enemies, now as if He were eagerly going to a festival. He is borne along on a strong tide of austere expectation and sublime resolution, silent but none the less impetuous.

As to what actually happened in Jerusalem in those momentous days, as to the inner history of that small circle of the faithful ones, question upon question remains which our records do not satisfactorily answer. But there is one sentence of Jesus which gives us a vivid picture of the whole situation. It is the key, as it were, to His mood and to His great hour; we feel that only supreme anguish could have forced it from Him: "If the people should hold their peace, the stones would immediately cry out." Despite its resemblance to the saying of Zechariah, this word accredits itself as a genuine and authentic word of Jesus. "If the people should hold their peace"—the assurance contained in these words makes it plain how Jesus came to allow the people to offer Him the greeting which they did on the occasion of His triumphal entry, and how it was He appeared before the City of Promises with an extraordinary claim. It explains to us why, when He was subjected to a serious attack on this account, He was wholly unwilling to yield by as much as a single step before His opponents. On the contrary, this word is proof that, full

of strength and mind made up, He proceeded
straightway to turn the tables on His opponents.
How deeply His soul must have been stirred, how
powerfully His heart must have glowed with the certainty that now the decisive hour for Jerusalem had
struck! How truly He must have believed that God
Himself had entered into their midst with grace and
judgment. How earnestly His soul must have been
aroused that He would call the very stones of the
street to witness against them—that He could feel
that even the stones, the hardest of objects and the
symbol of callousness itself, were in this hour permeated with tense anticipation!

In view of these claims, then, is a solemn entry
into Jerusalem as improbable as many critics have
supposed? Was it not a thing to be expected under
the circumstances? Is that entry really much more
startling an episode than the cleansing of the Temple, an incident which no critic doubts? That amazing act burst forth on the impulse of the moment
and was born solely out of an overwhelming sense of
the reality of God. The cleansing of the Temple?
Why, it was intended by Jesus to be the first in an
entire re-creation of all things from above! Such a
regeneration of mankind did not follow, and His bold
act remained but a fragment and a symbol; but how
complete were the fearlessness and the inner freedom of Jesus manifest in this unparalleled consciousness of authority! If these considerations be given
due weight, how can anyone doubt the fact of the
solemn entry?

It is hardly possible in our time to imagine with

at suspense the atmosphere of those days must
ve been charged. Jesus had forced his opponents
ito a desperate situation by making the claim that
He was the promised King of the people, and yet
not raising a finger against the unceasing arrogance
and oppression of the Roman rule. He was keeping Himself aloof from all politics, and yet He constituted in His Person a great political danger to
His people. After promising them an unheard-of
turn of fate, He Himself seemed to be simply waiting in vain from day to day for that cha   come.
Although He had gained public a   tioh,   He
was, in the eyes of the l   eckless dest   er
of the national unity oi   people. He was a
to point to many significant divine witnesses in His
favor, and yet He seems to lack decisive and indubi-
table authentication from God. While He was personally beyond reproach and suspicion, it was
equally true that He was at the same moment
endangering the safety of State and community.
Like the prophets of old, He was aglow with a rap-
turous passion for God—and yet, for all the leaders
could see, He was doing nothing at all to further
the world's progress by even a single move.

Let us try to grasp the mood of the best people
belonging to the groups opposed to Jesus. If we
wish to be fair to them, we must make an effort to
sense how they felt. For we know that only men
who were in the habit of trusting God without reservation, only men who possessed an inner receptivity for the Good and the Divine, could have
passed safely through the ordeal of fire to which

these men were being subjected by Jesus. For]
claims meant that they must decide without mu
time for forethought to take a stand by His sid
even though State, people, world, and everything
else might perish because of that choice. As Jesus
presented the matter, the alternatives were as clear
as the light of day; they would have to choose the
one or the other, and answer Yes or No. Never
had a people received a more radical challenge. Nor
would any other people have passed through the
ordeal of that choice in a more creditable way than
did the Jews. The tragedy of the situation did no
lie in the headstrong malice of a few purblind offi
cials, but in human nature itself. On the one side
stands a single divine personality, and on the other
a people who recoil from divinity so pure—who
are, indeed, incapable of welcoming it in its purest
form. Only when it is considered in this light and
the decision of the Jews construed as the decision of
humanity does the tragedy of Jesus rightly appear
to be the tragedy of God's intercourse with mankind.

The last days of Jesus in Jerusalem belong to the
sublimest memories of the human race. His thought
is fragrant with a freshness like unto the fragrance
and freshness of the dawn, and all the powers of
His highest person are completely mobilized. Raised
up to His full height, He faces His opponents and
easily frustrates their plots and their insinuations.
His whole nature lights up once more with the glow
of the conviction that He is able to enlighten their
ignorance, and He is cogent as never before.

The stories of the tribute-money, of the hope of

urrection, of the authority of the Baptist, and of
e adulteress will preserve the memory of that peak
f human sublimity to the end of time. With amazing vigor and power, when His enemies attack Him,
He instantly transforms Himself into the aggressor,
and when it is all over, He is left master of the
field. Quite undaunted, indeed, He proceeds on His
own initiative to seek them out, and runs his probe
to the very heart of their central dogma when he
asks them, "Whose Son is the Messiah?"

And yet it should always be remembered that this
same Jesus who can rise to the level of the superhuman is capable, nevertheless, of the tenderest
human solicitude. He trembles with despair as He
looks upon His disciples and sees their want of sensitiveness and strength of spirit; He implores them,
"Could you not watch with me one hour?" What
a mood of strange and almost depressing melan-
choly broods over the hours of His departure in
Bethany, over the supper of the Passover, and over
Gethsemane! Fully does Jesus let this mood express itself. He makes no attempt to conceal it
behind a cloak of impassive heroism. For, side by
side with this mood there is always another, a deep,
resolute, noble conviction as to His own mission.
His acknowledgment is so open that He depends
upon His disciples that His plea for their help
deeply moves us, and yet it is always accompanied
by a superlative gentleness and pity for their
pathetic insufficiency. His anguish over the spiritual blindness of His people is so poignant that it
makes us tremble, and yet His tenderness with them

never varies. There is in Him a solitary grande
of will in all His attitudes toward mankind, and a
the same time, is always undiminished, a childlike
trust in God. These moods move us as no poet
could ever move us, or make us feel how wonderful
these interwoven contrasts can be!

One morning Jerusalem awoke to find the news
spreading through the city like a running fire: "He
has been taken! He has already been sentenced!"
The higher officials knew well, indeed, just what
would follow. For, during the preceding days the
suspense over what action they were likely to take
had become almost intolerable. A sudden and complete change now took place in the mood of the
populace. A Messiah whom God would allow to
be taken captive and bound as a criminal was utterly
unthinkable to a Jewish populace, and a perfect fury
of disappointment spent itself upon the head of
Jesus. The Gospels have made the events of these
last hours intimately familiar to us. Even if historical investigation no longer permits us to accept
all the details as true, it leaves us the impression of
the monumental power and greatness of Jesus unimpaired. There is sufficient warrant remaining for
the acceptance of the view that the sentence against
Jesus was based upon no other ground than His
refusal to deny the claim to Messiahship. It can be
accepted as certain that He had to look on at what
seemed to be the complete collapse of all His work,
and to experience the full brunt of the ingratitude
and ill will of this populace for whose salvation He
had yearned more ardently and agonized more

deeply than had any other man. There can be no
question that He had to endure the betrayal and
cowardly flight of His "faithful ones," and to bow
to the total and brilliant victory which His enemies
felt that they had achieved. Never did a man appear
to suffer a more open, unconditional defeat. But the
victory which followed was no less complete—the
calm, silent victory of an unperturbed resignation.
While His refusal to take the proffered stupefying
drink is a seemingly minor act, really it is an unusually significant incident.

According to Mark, Jesus dies with this word on
His lips: "My God, my God, why hast thou for-
saken Me?" This dreadful cry, whose poignancy
pierces to the marrow in us, forces itself from
His soul with labored breath, like the last and
heaviest drop of blood from a heart crushed to death
falling to the ground. By no means is this cry to
be interpreted as the voice of despair and final dis-
illusionment. If that had been His mood, Jesus
would not have made use of an Old Testament word
within which lurks a hidden gleam of triumph. We
are made to feel here how Jesus, in the hour of His
utmost distress, as He casts about for a place where
His weary soul may rest, finds peace in this Old
Testament prophecy. When He recalls this verse
in one of the Psalms expressive of His own anguish
in all its height and depth, He feels no longer a
sense of banishment from the presence of God but
a return—like the Psalmist again—of His sense of
nearness to the living warmth of the control exercised by God over the issues of the world. Such was

His last thought, His farewell feeling in the flesh
But let us not dwell on the details. It is the whole
impression which they unite to make of His death
that is so unspeakably impressive and sublime. The
life that was so multitudinously active sinks down
into the complete inaction of silent suffering. The
masterful voice in speech becomes dumb in the stillness of death. The triumphant song of a great heart
which set out hopefully to win the world dies away
and is silenced in agony.

Let us picture to ourselves the ghastliness of His
death complete—the suspension of the dead weight
of His person from its pierced arms and legs, the
inflamed wounds, the long, drawn-out torment
induced by the distorted and swollen limbs, the vio-
lent stoppage of the circulation with all its attendant
feelings of nameless terror; the parching thirst under
the burning, pitiless sun, the hundreds of insect
stings. The witnessing of this acme of humiliation
on the one hand and the contrasting spectacle of the
silent and speechless resignation of Jesus would have
prostrated us. As long as our sensing of these hours
of horror shall remain acute, all crucifixes somehow
become paltry and superficial and all the hymns of
the Church effeminate and weak.

Let us now take one final glance at the last days
of Jesus. In vain do we try to describe the experience which our humanity passed through in His
person in those hours. A few short, penetrating
words upon the injustice of it all to His Judges, a
reply full of dignity defending His fundamental
integrity, a final avowal in which the meaning of His

whole life is brought majestically to a focus, and for
the last time hurled as a challenge to an unbelieving
world in language that is plain and definite, fearless
and sober, unpretentious and yet superlatively force-
ful—such is the last strong note on which the song
passes out. The rest is silence—breathless silence.

Agony, it is true, wrests one more cry from the
depths of His soul, but in it there is not one trace of
hatred, disillusion, or revolt.

And now a stillness heavily charged with signifi-
ance enfolds the cross, in which the greatest duel of
ur humanity is being fought out in His person.
Utter distress is struggling to win the day over purest selflessness. Agony and torment are doing their
worst to shake a will ready to carry trust to the point
of abnegation. Triumphing malice is taking the
offensive against tenderness that is divine. They
conquer not. The silence that envelops the cross
now suddenly becomes thicker still and of added
solemnity. In the angry sea of human sin the most
sublime of lives has gone down—but only as a pre-
lude to a glorious and triumphant victory on Easter
morn, imperishable forevermore.

Little more has been intended here than to sketch
this life in barest outline, which of all lives ever
lived by men touched the highest pinnacle of significance for our human world. So short it was in
years and yet so enduring in its effects, so abruptly
fractured and yet so wonderfully complete; so pre-
maturely checkmated and yet to the very end the
mighty affirmation of a will that knew no gainsay-
ing; so far away from us as history and yet so near

to us in spiritual experience; the object of ruthless
hostility almost without a parallel and yet the
blessed bringer to the world of endless joy.

Wherein lies the greatness of this life? What sur-
prising significance is there in it for us of a later
day? We ask in all soberness. Let it be observed
that we are not inquiring for the verdict of his own
generation, friend or foe. It is its ocean depth, the
secret of its strength and inspiration we are seeking
to fathom by getting as close as we can with our own
souls to the soul of Jesus. No beliefs or verdicts
the past can help us here, nor shall they, in ver
truth, be suffered to hinder. To be satisfactory, th
answer can be made only in terms of our own personal experience. And so we ask again, Wherein
resides that greatness?

In seeking an answer, we must remember that
Jesus invented nothing new, discovered nothing new.
He founded nothing and destroyed nothing. When
He died, the earth had undergone no external
change. It remained its same old self. The sick
whom He healed soon sickened again and died. The
words He spoke lived in a few simple hearts only.
Others, too, were soon credited with the performance
of the works which He had done. What He taught
in words can be found, if we search diligently
enough, in the utterance of others as well. Wherein,
then, lies His greatness?

The wondrous fascination which the life of Jesus
exerts over us is due, first and foremost, to the
stubborn impression which it makes upon us that it
is not the work of circumstance but the welling forth

of a remar̲ ʰˡᵃ and unique INWARDNESS. Extraordinary events a̲ ̲ ̲ ̲ ᵒᵗ lacking in the history
of His days, but it ̲ ̲ ̲ ̲ ̲ ̲ ̲ ̲ ̲ ̲ ̲ ᵣ which they
provide a fitting setting tha̲ ̲ ̲ ̲ ̲ ̲ ̲ ̲ ̲ ̲ y fascinates us and
wholly dominates our view. The life of no other
person known to history appears to flow so entirely
from an inward impetus, to be so basically under
the control of an internal necessity, as does the life
of Jesus. One feels almost as if it must be said that
His interior life had not reacted to but originated
ᵻs external counterpart. The call of John the
̦aptist, the thronging of the people without a shep-
̰erd, the hostility of His opponents, the quest for
̄ealth by the sick, the decisive struggles of the last
week, the final agony—all these seem but to provide occasions and opportunities for the inner life
of Jesus to project itself abroad and reveal its wealth
and quality. Nothing external left any mark on
Him, but the whole external world has come to bear
the imprint more and more of the quality of His
inner life. We do not mean to exaggerate; our char-
acterization is based on comparisons which we here
make between that life and the lives of Caesar or
Goethe, and even of Buddha. After these sober
comparisons we are constrained to ask, Where do we
find its fellow, another life word by word and deed
by deed so unmistakably gushing up out of the very
depths of its own inner nature, and remaining so
completely uncontaminated by outward circumstance? What other life from which whim and
caprice are so conspicuously absent? His is a life
that bubbled up copiously from unknown inward

deeps. Whenever it meets with obstacles, this life simply streams by them or cuts a channel for itself through them. It is not checked nor diverted from its course. The impetus of its power never seems to ebb.

How conspicuous is the lack of outward stimulus in the life of Jesus! Even to the simple education of His time He was almost a stranger. He met no men of remarkable character save John the Baptist, whom he seems to have instantly overshadowed. For all the competency with which we see Him equipped, He had nothing more to draw upon than the resources of His own inner life. Nor did the Old Testament dominate and bind Him; instead it awakened and stimulated His mind. Rather did His thought deal freely with it, dominate it, and feel perfectly at liberty to add to it. Friendship and domestic life, art and recreation—none of these was treated as essential by Him. He took from none and gave to all. It was natural that His unified spirit, His perfectly coördinated nature, rich in its own name, gloriously strong and with strength to spare, indeed, above all needs, should express itself in words and deeds. It was this inward abundance which lifted Jesus out of humblest obscurity, and its abiding singularity irradiates the centuries with a splendor peculiar to itself.

When this inward abundance sought outlet, it was taken in charge and held true to its course by a will royal in authority and steadfast in the execution of whatever is given into its keeping. Whatever Jesus might do, its genesis could be traced to

he same fundamental source. When He heals the
ick, and when He avoids them; when He retreats
before His enemies, and when He faces them; when
He limits His activities to the Jews, as well as when
He ministers to Gentiles; when He withdraws to an
obscure spot, and when He sets His face steadfastly
to go to Jerusalem; when He takes the scourge in
His hand, and when He offers the same hand to
receive the print of the nails—the same undeviating,
onsistent will courses through whatever He does,
rging from the depth of His soul, outpouring
n the wellspring of His life. This will seems to
and to overflow His every word and deed, or
ther all His words and deeds seem to be dyed
rough and through with its tincture. Whoever
or the first time catches the pure note of this will
sounding through the chords composed of the deeds
and words of Jesus is surprised and overwhelmed by
the answering echo of it which he also hears rever-
berating in his own soul. The life of Jesus is an
instrument that gives out this pure note, a tone
clear, voluminous, and sublime.

We think of other men of whom it can be said
that their lives bore evidence of a powerful will.
But it is in the very act of comparison with Jesus
that the highest point of mystery in this whole matter of the will discloses itself to us. Jesus had no
will of His own. His life has exerted an enormous
effect upon the course of human history; but His
will was not His own will—it was the unfailingly
obedient servant of an Over-will, a will beyond His
own. So unique was the onehood between these two,

His own and this Over-will, that only gradually has
the mystery of His life unveiled itself before the
eyes of men. The greatest injustice we could do to
Him would be to charge that disappointment over
not receiving the honor He expected led Him to com-
plain and threaten. Not one whit of personal desire
found welcome in His heart. But the desire of God
for the world was treated like the royal guest it is.
The only life that He would accept for Himself was
the one set for Him by the will of God; He asked
no other. He fixed upon no goal for Himself
adopted no resolution of His own devising, select
no wish of His own to realize; but from hour
hour He simply adopted deed after deed and wor
after word as they were announced to Him out o
the Will of God. For once in the history of mankind the Will Universal found the door wide open
by which to enter in its full purity into a human
being. And so there resounds through everything
Jesus does and says something that seems to come
from the deepest recesses of the mystery of the world
itself. Where can its like be found in all the story
of man?

Now this unique will lives and strives with all
the resources at its command for the salvation of
mankind. Even though Jesus did confine His work
to His own people, this was no sign that He was
lacking in desire for the salvation of mankind, but
rather was it done in the interest of such a wish and
its realization. He so deeply desired it, indeed, that
if it had been within the compass of His own will
to bring this salvation down from Heaven, He would
have done so.

Salvation, the salvation of the race complete—all His will is ever intent on this end as its goal; all His longing burns with this holy hope; His joys and sufferings, His expectations and apprehensions, all point toward this future as the needle to the pole. Here is a human personality that is possessed and filled to the brim throughout its entire range of willing, thinking, and feeling by an Over-will, and its aim is the highest salvation of mankind. A life endowed with a vigorous, indeed, an overvigorous , and yet that life is a selfless one; a life that insformed its native thirst for a life of its own to a selfless purpose to save and to heal, and yet life which remained in the living a perfectly human life—this was the life of Jesus. Whoever contemplates this life thus truly for the first time can hardly bear to turn his eyes away, so wonderful is the impression it makes upon him.

Do we claim too much when we say, as we contemplate His life in this way, that Jesus was the first man of us to feel what "living" means, what human life is meant to be, could be, and at its core really wants to be? Such a life would never drop down into a confused and aimless jumble of events and experiences; its life would perforce be rather a registration of its own inner will and purpose, the life of a personality coming forth to manifest itself like the sun at dawn from its hidden recesses below the horizon. It could never be such a conglomerate of deeds and passions and pain as chance might cast up, but the ongoing of a God-born spirit through human history—like the passage of the Gulf Stream through the ocean. Under these conditions a being would emerge on the human scene out of the world's mysterious background, its life unanalyzable in kind and unfathomable in richness, but capable of becoming visibly intertwined with the materials of external events and of weaving itself ineradicably into the texture of our world's history.

The life of Jesus makes us feel especially that there is a point in cosmic history where human life tends to exceed its previous bounds and become exalted to a plane of higher vision and understanding, and that anyone who is really anhungered and athirst for a true life must learn to let a Higher Being quicken and course through his being.

Life in its highest and best form of realization can come to us only out of the depth of the World-will itself—that is, out of the heart of God. The only true life open to us is this—the portion that is given to us day by day out of the sheer grace of the World-will.

Why not, then, let the wonder of that form of life thus unveiled for us in Him glow in our veins and shine in our eyes? Wherever power is at work creatively, there is life. Wherever soul and spirit in coöperation work creatively, there is human life. Wherever the highest spiritual and moral power of the universe is at work creatively, there is divine life. And this is the only true life. We see this life in Jesus. We do not need to question further. We do not need to turn this life into a theology, another theory. What we have discovered is a new, a free, joyous understanding of Jesus. And in doing so we have also discovered a new, a free, joyous understanding of human life itself. We perceive in Jesus the holy Unity to which the human spirit, permeated by the spirit of God, can and therefore must attain. It is given us to see in Jesus the sublime purity into which the human spirit can be transfigured by God's spirit. And Jesus also makes us to know how man can become, and should become, and does ever will to become, God, even as God ever wills to become man.

PART II
THE PERSONALITY

PART II

THE PERSONALITY

LET us thread our way back through the long
aisles of the centuries, get free and clear of the dull-
ing effect wrought by tradition, and then endeavor
to sense the real Jesus in our secret souls. In that
moment a world of high purity takes us into its
embrace. From this world a fully human voice
crosses over to us. It speaks to us in the person of
a genuine, full-panoplied humanity with an earnest
summons, given to no hesitations, and with a good-
ness that is unfathomable.

That, in general, is the nature of the first impression imparted to us by Jesus. Next, let us try a
slower approach to His nature, that from the outside. What do we know about His appearance, His
face and form? Nothing, nothing at all. Not even
the slightest account has been preserved as to how
this soul clothed itself in a fleshly lantern of vis-
ibility. Whoever wishes can interpret the accounts
to the extent of concluding that He could make a
deep impression when He appeared on the scene.
The money-changers in the Temple were hardly the
type of timid men to recoil so easily from an ordinary lone man. On the other hand, high officials
of the people and hundreds of other men emerged

without difficulty from His presence, unaffected by
the impress of His personality. Man after man met
and passed Him, saw and heard Him, and carried
away not even the remotest idea that world history
would say of this man the greatest and most divine
things.

That Jesus could heroically endure privations the
record here and there makes plain. He seems to
have needed less sleep than His disciples; He rises
while they all sleep. He is awake on the mountains;
He is still awake in Gethsemane. But the record
also says that He soon succumbs to the tortures of
crucifixion; and that Pilate, who was familiar with
such things, wondered that He died so soon. It
would scarcely be worth while to mention these details did they not serve best to illustrate how little
we know of Him physically. This alone seems to be
certain, that while His life demanded so much from
Him, His own body put few obstacles in his path
for Him to overcome. Then, too, the accounts of
the outflow of powers of healing compel us to infer
that His body was dominated by His spirit—the
body weakened but the spirit urged it on.

But what kind of spirit lived and ruled in this
body? It was the spirit of a prophet, and not the
spirit of a philosopher. Whoever tries to find in
the words of Jesus, which the first three Gospels
relate to us, an atmosphere of thinking in a state
of sublime calmness detached from the world such
as envelops the Dialogues of Plato and the works
of Spinoza—he seeks in vain. It is strange how many
philosophical questions are left untouched, even

some that one would think would crop up at every
step of the way for Jesus, and indeed almost block
His path.   How relate the omnipotence of God to
the freedom of men?   The love of God to the
power of evil in the living men?   How can God
in the final judgment sharply divide men simply
into good and bad?   How can God reply to the sins
of men in time with the torments of eternity in
punishment?   It is a marvel how little occasion
Jesus had to take up such questions as these in His
thinking and to illuminate them by His experience.
Perhaps these questions were neither in accord with
the spirit of the time nor congenial to the spirit of
the Jewish people, yet by helping us to say clearly
what Jesus was not, they pave the way to an exposition of what He was.

Calm reflection upon the forms of thought and
its enigmas was not one of His individual traits, but
certainly a deep insight into the nature of reality
was peculiar to Him.   His was that incomparably
great gift which we call religious intuition, through
which the individual mind feels itself in contact
with the mind of the world, and divines and under-
stands it as the mind of the child and the mind of
the father meet and are content.   Jesus did not do
His thinking in concepts, but in pictures which
reflected the nature of a thing just as the great sun
is reflected in a little mirror.   The single word
"Father" was such a sun-mirror by itself.   He did
not discover truths, but truths, wonderful for clar-
ity, He knew through experience.   He did not look
through the analyzing spectacles of logic, but per-

ceived everything, as it were, through the eyes of
the spirit itself; so He saw, as if He were standing
beside God and looking out, into the depths of true
and false devoutness. He did not pick His way
along the remote heights of pure thought; but He
lived in the heart of actuality and at the seat of the
mystery of the world. It was from this vantage
ground that He spoke of the invisible God who
makes His sun to rise upon the evil and upon the
good, and the rain to fall upon the just and upon
the unjust. Occasionally a strong persuasion visits
us that the Gospels in a flash of intuition have laid
bare to us how His great thoughts came to Him, as
the lightning flash which illuminates all from the
rising to the setting of the sun. His thoughts are
not the result of slow and painful processes of
thinking, but sparks of illumination marking the contact of His soul with the innermost nature of things.

His noblest words come forth as if the deep, divine
import of the occasion gave them birth and, as it
were, came to a consciousness of its own nature in
His pure mind. "Rejoice not that the spirits are
subject unto you; but rather rejoice, because your
names are written in heaven." "Who is my mother?
and who are my brethren?" "Whosoever shall do
the will of My Father which is in heaven, the same
is my brother, and sister, and mother." The holy
trace their descent not through the body given them
at birth but through the long line of "those who keep
the Words of God." Like gifts which His mind
appropriates immediately out of the depth of the
divine mind do such words appear as they circulate

among men. Thus to Jesus should be given not a
place among those who philosophize, but a place of
His own as the spokesman of philosophy itself. Life
to Him was not thinking, and thinking was not life,
as it is to so many great minds in history; but both
His thinking and His life were photographs of the
divine mind dwelling in Him, which also lived for
Him in everything else. Harmoniously and organ-
ically His life and thinking poured forth from the
fundamental will of His nature.

It is a delight to contemplate His mind in its
manifold, delicate shadings: intellectual penetration
is there which can delve into the inner life of things
and men, and detect in a person a yearning desire
to accept as well as a contrary disposition to reject;
mental power which compels thought to clothe itself
in attractive form; intellectual sagacity which
knows so very certainly how to distinguish appearance from reality, as in His tart descriptions of
Pharisaic devoutness; mental daring which does not
hesitate to set the truth before the soul in a one-
sided way that cannot be forgotten or confused, as
in the Sermon on the Mount; mental stature which
cleaves its way in the most critical moment to some
really great word, a word not subject to embarrass-
ment nor brooking denial, which with convincing
assurance "strides into their midst and passes on,"
as in debate with the Pharisees; mental delicacy
able to catch the stirrings and emotions of the soul
and reduce them to such tender, incorrupt, and
almost transparent expression, as in the parables of
the Lost Son and the Merciful Samaritan; mental

explosiveness which bursts like an irresistible storm
upon His opponents, as in the invocation of those
woes against the leaders and deceivers of the people.

An exceedingly fortunate combination of mental
qualities was at His disposal for His work within
the world's history; what He did not have was no
loss, for it would have diverted Him; what He
needed He had in abundance. That coördination of
mental powers which He possessed gave out, however, a very singular tone of joy and elevation. And
this fortunate gift of inner harmoniousness was the
source of an innermost, moral, indispensable power
which permeated in a sovereign way all His other
gifts.

The mind of Jesus is the vestibule to His character. No thought-out ideal of perfection meets us
there in which the virtues are laid, the one beside
the other, like colors on a palette; but a man, a
complete man, possessed of a constitutional vitality
which lights up His qualities as sunshine sets a
many-colored window ablaze. The native character
of Jesus manifests itself most conspicuously in a
keen, pronounced, and unusually vivid sensitiveness.
The Gospels share with us experiences in which feeling many a time impetuously wells up and passionately seeks outlet. At His first allusion to the
approaching sufferings, when Peter offers with obviously friendly good will his well-meant wisdom, he
has to bear with the abrupt, stern word: "Get thee
behind me, Satan . . . for thou savorest not the
things that be of God, but those that be of men."
No doubt this rebuke seems to us to be too stern.

But in that day all the world was convinced that evil powers were able to enter into a man and speak through him at any moment, Peter could rightly feel alarmed and at the same time not primarily to blame; he could feel the word of rebuke to be not only proof that all was not right with him but also a beneficial warning. Yet this word is vivid evidence of how pronouncedly the emotional life of Jesus could change temperature, how strongly an unexpected act taking Him by surprise from the side where He sought His companions could affect Him, and how passionately His acute sensitiveness was inclined to revolt against His suffering.

Still stronger objection is raised by many people to the energy with which Jesus stood out against the Pharisees than to His reply to Peter. Did these Pharisees not also desire the best and seek it diligently in their own way? Did He not do them an injustice? Did they deserve the centuries of contempt which have rested heavily on them since the judgment of them spoken by Jesus has served to obscure all that was worthy of praise in them? We feel no call to act as defending counsel for Jesus; but it may be well to recall how things stood. The high duty fell to the lot of Jesus of fighting, not against the Pharisees, but against false piety. And that gave Him a sacred right to condemn where to others the task of judgment would not have been appropriate. Its justification lies in facts like these: His whole life-work depended for results upon His success in opening men's eyes to the abuses of old authority; His perception must have been unusually keen of how dissembling, half-heartedness, and vain pride are the most dangerous enemies of God, and that, therefore, a heavier responsibility rested on Him than on them. His graciousness in the beginning and His silent composure at the end attest to what an extent the imperatives of an objective struggle, and not personal sensitiveness, controlled Him. Not only do these considerations support His right to condemn what the Pharisees stood for in His eyes, but much more does the fact that when they most injured Him personally He remained completely non-combatant. However, common knowledge tells us that there is, indeed, no greater enemy of the Divine than conceited forms of piety, which, under the cover of self-complacency, choke and kill all power of receptivity for the true sense of the Divine. The only help for such people is a crushing blow given to their fictitious lordliness. Mankind would be much farther away from veracity and from truth if the passionate zeal of Jesus against all specious conceit and hypocrisy had not been at work all through history.

But those who regret now and then the passion to which the vitality of Jesus could rise might well stop to consider all that we owe to it. We owe to it the great hour of outburst in the Temple, when Jesus, shaken by the profanation in full fling around him, puts no check upon the outraged feelings surging up within Him, but rather lets the deeply moved tide of His emotions have free exit, regardless of consequences to Himself, in an act of impressive power. To it we owe also the wonderful outgoings of His soul toward sinners, as the story of Zaccheus witnesses, where a single yearning look cast upon Him from the midst of the crowd awakens the deepest compassion and stirs to action the strongest impulses of mercy in His whole nature. He never stops to consider the nature of the comment His visit to that home will provoke nor the prejudices it may create against His cause, and He is forgetful of His own previous resolution not to make any stay in Jericho. We owe to this same passionate vitality the majestic heroism of many a saying of Jesus in which the powerful glow of the mood that gave it utterance lives on for all time: "And if thy right eye offend thee, pluck it out, and cast it from thee." And we owe those tender scenes to it where Jesus, in spite of the hate of men and the distresses of the time, opens His soul to the glory of a wild flower, or to the noble possibilities that slumber in the soul of a child. We owe to this flaming intensity of soul the formidable arguments which Jesus uses in debate with His critics, born of the innermost mood of the moment; and we owe to it, likewise, His transport of joy when He saw the widow standing at the offering-box, giving her mite. We owe to it the full, free insight into life which speaks to us in the parables of Jesus, as well as in poignant, sublime hours like those in Gethsemane. Always did Jesus merge Himself into what was going on at the moment, purely and unreservedly subjecting Himself to the occasion with all its demands; or, rather, the moment merged itself into Him, developed in His presence like a beautiful blossom, achieved out of the rich and full life of His soul a divine flow ering.

If the way be studied in which the soul of Jesus expresses itself, the puzzle is whether to wonder more over the ebullience of His emotion or its purity, the responsiveness or the impartiality of His sensitiveness. How fully and freely does He give way to the sorrow of His impending death in Gethsemane, nobly unconcerned over what His disciples may see fit to think of a Master and Messiah whom they see disheartened and not hesitating to implore God's mercy. Only He who has nothing to conceal can thus open His nature to men down to its very depths. Had not Jesus' consciousness of Himself and of His mission been opalescent in its sincerity, this habit of total absorption into the moment would have been unthinkable. As it is, it gives us ever-renewed delight to observe how objects, men, and events, one after another, rap at His soul, and then how His uniquely sublime soul answers them all with genuine understanding sympathy.

Especially should we not fail to notice how Jesus escapes the menace of the dangers incident to a vivid emotion. Not always does the spirit keep firm hold of the reins in its dealings with feeling. So when the feelings, after a spell of roaming, come back under the domination of the mind again, all kinds of unpleasant things, it soon appears, have happened for which allowance has to be made. Nothing of the sort do we meet in Jesus. His emotional life gives us the impression of being spiritually illuminated. Thus it comes to pass again and again that His

·eplies could not have been uttered more happily
even had they been the product of the most subtle
reasoning. And yet they are alive with the full,
spontaneous, fresh life of His soul.

A clearer instance would be hard to conceive than
the story of the woman taken in adultery, which,
strange to say, does not appear in the manuscripts
until the third century. Nevertheless, it is certainly
to be attributed to Jesus and to no one else. "Master, this woman has been taken in the act of adultery; Moses has commanded us in the Law to stone
such a guilty one. What do you say?" Jesus is
silent, due perhaps to a feeling of indignation at
the brutality of this censor of morals, who would
make the downfall of a human being the occasion
of a public dispute and, moreover, turn her predica-
ment, difficult as it is already, into a shameful trap.
Or Jesus is silent, perhaps, through compassion for
this woman that she should be baited for her error
to provide amusement for a crowd; or again His
pausing may be due to hopeful anticipation that the
woman's sense of modesty will show through her
shame. But even then when He speaks it is only
one sentence: "He that is without sin among you,
let him first cast a stone at her." And no man in
the world could have spoken at·this critical moment
a more fortunate piece of counsel. It disarmed the
accusers, stirred the consciences of the bystanders,
humiliated the heroes of virtue, ended the debate,
destroyed the trap, dispersed the crowd, and saved
the woman.

And by an advance beyond this Law of Moses

which has not been called in question, towering preeminence has been given to the greater commandments of self-knowledge and of forgiveness. Moreover, by leaving Jesus Himself standing unassailably superior to His enemies, it has opened a way for Him into a human heart whom He wishes to help. We can only faintly conjecture the extent of the resources of soul of one who can achieve so much with a single sentence. But even the act of conjecturing is itself an experience of inmost exaltation. Such a transforming word, we would ordinarily assume, was the outcome of long cogitation and subtle reflection. Yet the whole life of Jesus—His inmost self—is contained in that, so that from it as from nothing else we have learned to know Him truly. The light cast by Jesus' soul at its maximum shines in this sentence, instead of being toned down by refraction through the medium of reasoned thought and deliberation, and yet its purport could not be better expressed by the hardest intellectual labor. Deepest emotion wells up in unrestrained power and in uninterrupted flow, but it flows in channels of high-wrought thought which a mind, marvelously firm in its tread, puts at its service, as it were, instinctively.

Scarcely less remarkable than this interplay of feeling and intellect in Jesus is the corresponding relationship of feeling and will. Vivid emotions easily swerve the will of men out of the channel chosen for it. The will of Jesus flows along in a current so broad and deep in the interior of His being that all the play on its surface and any momentary agita-

tion, however turbulent, is sure to be brought under
restraint and subdued by the main stream. Complete absorption in the moment, and strong, steady
persistence in striving for a far-away goal, incom-
patibles ordinarily, seem in Him securely united.
Here, again, an incident may serve as enlightenment
—the story of the tribute-money. "Is it right for
us to pay tribute unto Caesar or not?" We know
that this question is a compound of finesse and
malice, intended to trap Jesus whichever way He
turns. However He might answer, He seems to be
lost. Nevertheless He breasts His way to a splendid triumph past all the pitfalls in His path: "Render therefore unto Caesar the things of Caesar; and
unto God the things that are God's." Again it seems
the choice of words must be the result of hours of
thought and deliberation; again delicate sensitiveness to all the demands of the moment is in evidence; but mightiest of all, the weight is discernible
of a very powerful, divine will. That Jesus could
then and there deliver to these opponents an admon-
itory sermon, and so soon convert their question
should one pay tribute to Caesar into a question of
conscience, namely, should they have discharged the
tribute of devotion due from them to God, that He
does not seem to be thinking at all of Himself nor
of victory; that He brings home to them the urgency
of their obligation to God with the force of a revelation, and in the twinkling of an eye compels them
to recognize the reason of their bondage to the
Romans, the incompetence and hollowness of their
leaders, and the depth of the chasm thus interposed

between them and Him; that He compels recognition from them of the super-worldly spirit of His Messiahship and the magnitude of His demands in the name of God. None of all this would have been possible except the will of God in its unsullied purity had been wrought into the groundwork of His nature.

This single, firmly intrenched principle of His life is like a deep, clear organ tone upon which the feelings of the moment build like a composer noble melodies, rich, free, and resonant. Insight into the life of Jesus begins when one learns to listen to these holy harmonies. After this point has been attained much else begins to be clear. It can now be understood how it was that Jesus could so freely become absorbed in every little neighborhood joy and still make people feel the momentous earnestness of His life; how the keenest sympathy could be shown by Him to those in sorrow and yet the conviction remain that eternal tranquillity was His own estate in life. Also, we realize how the heart of Jesus beats with the purest compassion for every distress without blunting our acute sense of the austere grandeur back of it; how a full and ever-present comprehension of all weakness and sin is shown to be not incompatible with that wonderful fragrance of purity disseminated by the whole life of Jesus; and, finally, it enables us to recognize how the finest degree of sensitiveness may direct the choice of words without marring the ring of truth given out by them.

We truly believe that in saying all this we have

not added anything to nor exaggerated anything in Him, but have confined ourselves simply to what we see plainly. As the study of His natural character proceeded, already His moral character, shining through distinctly, was everywhere perceptible. Now let us regard still more closely this light of moral influence that radiated from Him. A light cannot be described by analyzing it into its separated colors; an account must be given of its action and power. So we do not tally off virtue after virtue and seek to find them in the life of Jesus, but rather undertake to observe the ways in which the living man responds to the demands of life. One distinctive reaction must be mentioned in advance. When the call to His work comes to Him, Jesus appears before men an inwardly perfected being, memorably so. His whole strength and His whole effort was dedicated to the welfare of His people. Against weaknesses of His own, as far as we can see, He did not have to battle. The great struggles that go on within Him are concerned with the right comprehension of the will of God, as the story of the Temptation shows, and over right obedience to the will of God, as Gethsemane testifies. These conflicts never center around any evil in His own breast. Even those who think that this freedom from the common necessity to checkmate evil impulses makes Jesus a stranger to earthly things and remote from mankind cannot question the fact, unwelcome as they find it. They may remind us, perhaps, of the saying: "Why callest thou me good? None is good save one, that is, God." But this saying, by itself alone, can never prove the presence of the consciousness in Jesus' bosom of inner conflict with sin. Jesus, it may be, was here disapproving the employment of a word so weighty in content as part of a polite formula, from a desire to have so great a word reserved for the purity of God alone which is untouched even by conflict. It is certain in any case that He did not mean to signify a consciousness of personal lapses.

Jesus displays the most delicately sensitive powers of moral perception, as, for example, in his affirmation that a man who is unreconciled with his brother is not fit to offer to God even the smallest gift at the altar. His keen moral susceptibility is shown again in His appraisal of a worship of God attended by a cherished feeling of complacency as futile. The austerity of moral will shown in His interpretation of even a covetous look at a woman as adultery is sublime. Nevertheless, no suggestion appears of any lapses of His own, no recollections of personal defeats, no awareness of evil desires, no thought of His own unworthiness, no depression over a sense of personal insufficiency—and not even once a word of thanks to God for grace unmerited when His awareness of His high mission is most intense. Can it be that we owe these omissions in this portrait of Jesus to the reporters? No, for a living picture so full of life could not conceivably have had its blemishes erased without losing the freshness of its original coloring.

And yet it is not enough to name over the blemishes from which Jesus was free. What He was, is

r us even better attested and more fruitful in
esults. We shall therefore now observe how the
demands that life makes upon men came to Him
one after another in order to discover what manner
of being He is. When the message of God which
John. was preaching came to His ears, it brought to
Him, too, the command: "Leave thy father's house
and go into a land which I will show unto thee!" It
is true that Buddha detached himself no less completely from all his old associations and he could
afterwards meet his former wife and treat her as if
she were altogether a stranger to him. But just
the opposite is the human greatness and joyousness
of Jesus, for He retains His love for those from
whom He has won His freedom. He leaves home
at the behest of His commission to devote Himself
to His Gospel, and yet He continues to feel Himself
attracted to homes like the one at Bethany and to
find joy in them. And when His own people reject
Him, no lament and no accusation fall from His
lips, but only the free and untroubled words: "A
prophet is not without honor, save in his own coun-
try, and in his own house." So He lives a homeless
life, and yet continues to love homes. For all the
joys of family life, also, Jesus preserved a fully receptive attitude. He loved to look into the eyes of
children and He knew how to relate affectionately
holy things concerning a father's heart. And yet it
is this same Jesus who speaks the imperturbable,
searching words: "Who is my mother? and who are
my brethren? Whosoever shall do the will of my
Father which is in heaven, the same is my brother,

and sister, and mother." A point of vantage above
the world, coupled with open hospitality to its
appeals, both alike genuine and strong, so completely different and yet so closely allied—how striking the impression they make!

Although His liberation from home ties is inex-
orably final, the price, however, has to be paid daily
in privation. Steady wandering from town to town,
comfortless night's lodgings in a boat or under the
trees, nourishment barely enough to sustain Him,
such as the fig tree by the wayside or the ears of
grain in the field offered—this was the lot of Jesus.
Many another, to be sure, has endured similar privations; but to have said so little about them—and
that little so large-heartedly—scarcely anyone has
equaled Him in this respect. Only two incidental
references to His lot come from the lips of Jesus.
"The foxes have holes, and the birds of the air have
nests; but the Son of Man hath not where to lay
his head." This spoken to one who desires to follow Him! In choosing the loss of family life to
represent the heavy sacrifice which becoming His
follower would entail, Jesus showed how He valued
home comforts and begrudged them to none, but also
how, nobly and voluntarily, He chose homelessness
for Himself. Nothing of self-pity, nothing of self-
adulation do we find in this utterance. Back of this
free renunciation is perfect peace. Whoever weighs
this renunciation in the scales of Nietzsche's heart-
rending poem, "Woe to him who has no home!"
must instantly be sensible of its grandeur. The second, also, was spoken in behalf of others, the ques-

tion to the disciples at the end of their life together:
"Have you ever had lack of anything?" with their
reply, "Lord, never!" Vibrant here once more is
the memory of those days of wandering, so eloquent
of renunciation and privation, that became trans-
muted into gratitude and trust in God.

Every vocation has its own peculiar temptation.
Whoever passionately yearns for what is purest sees
ever confronting him the danger of tolerating, for
the sake of victory for the cause, the use of ways
and means which, anything but pure in themselves,
seek to borrow a cloak of purity from the cause
which they plead to serve. Every great reformer
has succumbed to this danger: even Luther con-
sented to the bigamy of the Landgrave, Philip of
Hesse, because of his powerful support of the Ref-
ormation. No admiration can be too strong, therefore, for the purity with which Jesus kept His divine
work free from the smirch of evil devices and
machinations. Not for a moment did He permit
Himself to accept a man's enthusiasm for Him as a
substitute for His own moral improvement. He
eschewed completely the allegiance that could be
won by personal gifts, and, instead, sought to win
men through His one all-inclusive gift as God-re-
vealer. He avoided, wherever He could, any act
which would add to the dazzling power of His fame
and interfere with the power of salvation in His
words. He demanded a clear-cut decision in favor
of His cause and not of Himself from men. When,
at the last, the decision was plainly going against
His cause, He went down with it, although half a

compromise would have saved Him, and perhaps
even have raised Him to exalted station. Wherever
the struggle took Him, He kept struggling to maintain unsullied His fidelity to His mission—in the
desert of temptation, when He first visualized
clearly the purport of His commission; on the mountain, when it seemed that His work might lead, if
He so willed, to the splendor of a royal crown; in
Gethsemane, where His mission seemed to be fad-
ing away into darkness and oblivion. To-day His
fidelity to His mission stands forth in all its illu-
minating purity, producing an indescribable effect
of moral majesty and sublimity. He withstood His
temptation to compromise. He carried out a divine
commission which had to be performed entirely
among men, entirely for the sake of men, and yet
be kept unspotted from profanation by men.

And we must note not only the taint from which
He kept Himself free, but also how thoroughly
He remained true to Himself. All the power
required for the fulfillment of His work must be
found in His own inner resources. Friends? They
proved to be devoid of understanding and unreliable,
and remained so. How it must have taxed Him to
perceive this in such an unblinded way as Jesus saw
it all, and then to overlook it without bitterness as
Jesus did! A weighty prediction, an earnest warning, with an untroubled kindness through it all—
no other did they ever experience from Him. And
the people? Stolidly they gazed like strangers at
all that was done in love of them and for their good.
With moving earnestness Jesus predicted the conse-

quences of this denseness, and with grave concern he pondered their want of insight and initiative, but no exasperated, no embittered, no disgusted word came to His lips. The magnitude of His sadness can only be measured by the greatness of His love; it was even born out of the greatness of that love. And His enemies? How much human impurity had His purity to face? how much human pettiness and baseness had His larger scope to reckon with? Of all that we learn, indeed, very little. But still, with this in mind, it is worth while to look into the accounts we have: no weakness and no wavering, no duplicity and no flinching or equivocation, no secrecy and no half-mindedness, not one word or deed which falls short of full height in spiritual stature is discoverable in Jesus, as far as our eyes can still penetrate into the records. Who can dispute this statement successfully? In freest contact He lives among men; with utter fearlessness He makes His challenging advances to them. He never speaks to less than their whole power, never demands less of a man than the gift of mind, body, and soul to God. Solitary He maintains His stand above the whole world on the heights of His unique claims. What a spectacle of inward power and inward poise for us to contemplate!

But the last and greatest tempter was still to be reckoned with—God Himself. He let Him be carried into the thickest gloom and be asked: "Do you still hold fidelity to your commission fast?" Jesus had done all for God—and God still asks more and does nothing for Him. Jesus had given all His strength to the Kingdom of God—and now when His life reaches its nadir, there is no Kingdom of God, no glimmer of it, indeed, however dim, in compensation of His all. He must face unmitigated outward failure and still retain intact an inner certainty of victory. When mobbed by the triumphant forces of evil, He has to preserve His best from harm and indeed prove how excellent it is. The dreadfulness of this ordeal fails to annihilate completely His presentiment that His agony is going to help prepare the salvation of the world—it thus serves to bring out the greatness of His faith. The terrible gloom of abandonment by God is His end. God refuses to answer His questions—and, in doing so, asks Him in the most telling way for the reply of His innermost nature to that refusal. And His fidelity stands fast. All the shuddering and temptation to hesitancy He experiences do not retard His decision to hold out for even an hour. He is on hand, He is ready, He is willing as soon as He becomes convinced that He has learned God's inflexible, "I will it." He whose nature was living emotion and vigorous action in consenting consents fully and becomes a man of silent endurance, so completely a passive sufferer that the centuries since have seen nothing else in their portrait of Him.

Is it exaggeration to say that here is an exhibition of moral strength which proved itself equal to the maximum strain, yea, superior to it? Power is measured by the resistance which it can overcome. Name a power that could have overcome Him. What form of temptation was there left to send out against Him for His further proving? He who has ever been possessed by a vivid perception of this superiority to infidelity in His life, needs no doctrine of the sinlessness of Jesus to instruct him. His own soul perceives other things and better things than this doctrine can offer him in this genuinely human life and striving. One of these is the strongest moral will that he ever encountered.

After all, the unique glory is the perfect fusion of Man and Commission, of Commission and Man, so luminously presented to us. Where else in the world can a parallel instance be pointed out? We see only unbroken harmony: the tasks which go with the Commission are fulfilled without friction and the gifts possessed by the Man completely fulfill themselves in the work of executing His Commission. Nowhere does the Commission exceed the Man, and nowhere does the Man exceed the Commission— nothing but unity, the noblest unity, a unity between the two dwelling on the heights! It is as if we were looking on at morality incarnate. We are in dread of exaggerating and equally in dread of falling short of reality; but is it not really true that here or nowhere morality itself, and yet a genuine man, also, and a warm human life, are on view? Pray, can all this be invention or distortion? Why has such a portrait been drawn nowhere else than in our homespun Gospels?

But not yet have we passed the last gate of the sanctuary. We have not yet entered the Holy of Holies. Underneath the moral character of Jesus, however, we have already been able to detect attractive glimpses of His religious nature. Now the time has come to dwell in contemplation on that innermost Life. Our records contain a saying which we are compelled to acknowledge a genuinely authentic and quite original saying of Jesus, since there is no one else capable of uttering it and no one since who was willing to take it seriously. When the father of a sick boy appeals to Him: "If thou canst do anything, have pity upon us and help us," Jesus answers: "If thou canst? To him who believes, all things are possible." Such startling words repeatedly sprang from His soul to His lips. In the hearts of His disciples, men of little faith, a similar saying which He once spoke to them has also been preserved: "If ye have faith as a grain of mustard seed, ye could say unto this mountain, Remove hence to yonder place; and it shall remove." May not such sayings take us nearest to the innermost principle of the life of Jesus just because they pour forth so audaciously and recklessly on the spur of the moment? To what conclusion would this lead? In that event, Jesus must have found access to a reservoir of life in Himself so powerful that the world ceased to be its substantial self and could by Him be made over new. He would then have been conscious that this superabundance of power in Himself was insurgently strong enough to make him feel as if the powers of creation stirred within Him, and as if the breath of the Creator of the world was in Him, eager to go forth once more.

On Luther's monument in Worms we read the word: "Faith is nothing else than the real, true Life in God Himself." Never has a man come nearer to sensing what faith was for Jesus than this same Luther. Not he who is merely openly receptive to the word of God likes the life of faith, but he who is attached to God, nature to nature; not he who has confidence in God but he who is in God's confidence—we had almost said, he who is wedded to God by all He is and all He has; not he who fixes his gaze upon the divine, but he upon whom the divine is focused so that it streams into his life, unconditioned and unhindered. That life is the life of faith. Jesus led that life. We have seen in our study of Jesus how freely He dares to take the direction of His life from God alone. Effortlessly and copiously His life actually streams forth out of God's will for it. A feeling of happiness hides at its core and darts hither and thither at times as if it were uncontrollable—waves of energy feeling strong enough to cope with the whole world. "Nothing will be impossible unto you." All this strength, however, is strictly held in the hollow of God's will. However impetuous the flood, it does not overflow its bounds but remains within the bed appointed it of God, be that channel ever so limited. Confined, obedient, that powerful stream of life goes on its way, a way determined for it by a Holy Will. Nowhere, indeed, do the counsel and life of Jesus seem to stand so at odds as in His promise that all petitions to God will be answered, and the fact that petition to God is so rare in His personal practice. It is as if He carried within Himself the assurance of access to power enough to do all that He was

directed and at the same time the will to endure all
that He was called to suffer. We are standing here
in the presence of the holy secret of His Life. All
things are possible for Him in this union with God,
and all impossible, were that union to be broken.
The purity of His devotion to God is equivalent, and
perhaps the open door of access, to the abundance of
His power from God.

In this exquisitely beautiful balance the nature
and the life of Jesus hold themselves poised. When
the one pole, "It must be thus!" is reached, the
other must be called to mind, "He who has faith
can do all things!" for the survey of that life to be
complete which was passed in an imposing equipoise
between a consciousness of power and a passion of
fidelity, inimitable in its beauty.

Nor was the vitality of Jesus tireless. It was subject to the common rhythm of periods of action and
of rest. After giving a flume its head, the gates
need to be shut and the water impounded in a still
sea before it can rush on as before to its work. Concealed from our view are the hours in the life of
Jesus when He retires to God from a period of activity to renew His life with fresh stores of its original
power from God, as if it would take breath out of
God's deeps for a new lease of unconquerable life.
All we know is that Jesus gave much time to God
alone, however much time He might have granted
to men. And we receive numerous intimations that
He returned to the world always with a wonderful
access of solemnity of spirit, as if He were sent anew
from God. He was in that newly surcharged state

when He came down from the mountain, and His disciples, under the stimulus of the impression it made upon them, broke out almost involuntarily with the request, "Master, teach us how to pray!" Similarly when after the feeding of the multitudes and the refusal of a kingly crown He disappeared into the darkness of the night, only to return after long hours to His disciples, it was as if in the interval he had to their astonishment been imbued by God Himself with a confidence which was superhuman. Again, when He rose to His feet from the deepest agony of His life in Gethsemane and went to encounter His enemies, His temper was so solemnly resolute and elevated that, as if overcome by the presence of the unspeakably holy, they fell back at first as from a conqueror.

Perhaps we have already transgressed the limits beyond which the use of our divining rod is inappropriate. But what would we not give for just one hour of mere propinquity to Him and to what He felt in those holy nights beneath the stars on the mountains of Galilee! There contact was established and the World received the life of God. There the mystery which is God sank into a soul which had removed the last layer of self to receive it. In those hours, the all-loving will of God for men entrusted itself to a heart which had emptied itself of every wish other than to submit to its leading, and to that alone. But why ask more than we possess? For the light which began to burn in the depths of the soul of Jesus in those sacred star-lit nights is still reflected clearly in His words and deeds. This is how things stood with Jesus: His belief was not a light received for His own guidance but for transmission to others. Its rays flame up powerfully in the words of the Sermon on the Mount, and glow with gentle serenity in the parables; again they glorify the daily scene—the sparrow on the roof and the flower in the field. The rays of that sun can pierce the distance to the end of the world and the Judgment; they can come streaming in, bringing pure kindness and joy with them into a sinner's heart; they can act as a searchlight to alarm the conscience of the hypocrite; and they can throw a glamour over the everyday life. On rare occasions, with a burst of brilliance as if it could not be contained in His inner life, this sun shows us the full glory of its own splendor out of sheer thankfulness and rejoicing. It is at all times the one pure light which proceeds not from Him as from a mirror but which lives in Him so thoroughly at home and in such free play that we feel it to be the native core of His Being.

We would like now to consider the religious life of Jesus from another side. In Him are united the keenest susceptibility to God that we know, and also the strongest conceivable passion actively to take sides with God. God companions Him within and without; in the rain as well as the sunshine; in the germinating of the seed in the field and the heart of the shepherd who carries homeward his exhausted lamb; in the monetary impulse of the woman disciple who anoints His head and in the black betrayal which precipitates His death. And

in the degree that He thus reacts to God, in that
same degree does He feel how harsh and painful is
the ungodliness of mankind. The sour countenance
of a guest at a feast is just as intolerable to Him as
the bargaining of the hucksters in the Temple of
Peace; as is also the much speaking of a man at
prayer and the sacrificial gift of a man unreconciled
to his brother. His hearing, which is so sharp at
catching every whisper which God speaks to His
soul, is the source of His indignation toward every
form of impurity encountered by Him on the road.
Susceptibility to God—and fidelity to God! Wherever He recognizes God, either in an external event
or in an inner precinct of His own nature, Jesus
takes God's side, as if that were a matter of course,
as if nothing else were at all possible. From facts
like these arises an impression of a life on its way
from God to men and not as it is with men even of
great faith, a life on its way from men to God. One
cannot be sure whether Jesus clasps God's hand or
God clasps His, but only that their hands are joined.
His response to God's will waits not on any resistance to be overcome but establishes itself immediately as an inner power of life.

To be shut out from God—the thought of it
would have been for Him a horror. What deep
joys must He have experienced in God's intimacies!
And as all Jesus aimed at in everything that He did
was to have it serve as a channel for the will of
God, so He accepted everything that befell Him
as traceable to the will of God. "Thou couldest
have no power at all against me, except it were given

thee by consent from above"—this saying from th
Gospel of John expresses a Gibraltar-strong sense o
God's overcontrol of human affairs that is beyond
disturbance—a mood in which the soul of Jesus is
immersed even in its suffering. His business is not
with enemies filled with hate, but with God who is
extending a cup to His lips and bestowing a baptism upon Him. Even the conspirings of His enemies against His life do not appear to Him to have
anything to do with His death; that is the carrying
out of a resolution which He Himself makes. As
His own act His death becomes ennobled, and the
crucifixion also which His enemies desire in their
rage is the servant of His own freely chosen course.
A more exalted decision in favor of coalescence with
the will of God both in action and in suffering cannot be imagined. To speak in modern language, in
the person of Jesus we meet the prince of religious
radicals. Only on the purest possible fulfillment of
the divine will and the most unreserved devotion to
it does Jesus set his mind. To lose touch with God
is His only fear, to glorify God before men His only
desire. We do well to recall two sayings of our
time: one by Carlyle, "Religion is an heroic form
of living"; and the other by Nietzsche, "Who is a
hero? Whoever serves a great cause in such a way
that all consideration for himself is forgotten." In
the exalted atmosphere of the high regions which are
indicated here, Jesus went up and down the world.
No reference points to any gradual ascent up to this
height on His part, but He is presented as moving
about freely in these altitudes, from the days of

oneliness in the wilderness of Judea to the day of
His avowal of His coming death as He stood ringed
about by triumphant enemies.

Keenness of sensibility and steadfastness of will,
the two qualities which we named earlier as natural
gifts in Jesus, appear here again in action as susceptibility to God's presence in His vicinity and
fidelity to His decision to take God's side. They
shine and glow in their transfigured perfection. Or,
rather, the divine irradiates them. As if dedicated
solely to the one noblest end, they serve only to
make the divine visible. His sensibility finds out
through its delicate powers of response what God is;
His strong, steady will clings to what God desires
of Him. The life of Jesus began and ended in religion. In His fidelity to His decision to side with
God the holy God came to live in the presence of
men; in His susceptibility to God's encircling presence the God of kindness came and dwelt with men.
Thus Jesus was, as it were, predestined to become
the standard-bearer of the highest revelation of God
before the centuries, the transmitter of the news of
His holy love. With a taken-for-grantedness and a
sense of security almost blinding to look upon, His
being rests in the arms of a God of pure kindness,
and the God of pure kindness rests thoroughly at
home in His reposeful, strong, luminous, capacious
nature. Such hours as Gethsemane only serve to
remove all doubt and to protect our portrait of Him
from any semblance of phantom or shadow, and keep
it fully human.

Son of God? . . . What does the choice of a word

matter after the reality has now been vouchsafed
to us!   Still, if the attempt has to be made to
compass this reality in one word, no better word
will be found.   Only it must not be understood in the
sense of a doctrine, but in the living, historical sense
of His time: the Son of God is He upon whom rests
the Father's pleasure, to whom is entrusted the
Father's work.   So we dare say that Jesus did not
indeed appropriate this name to Himself, but sensed
it in a flash as the truth of His being, accepted it so
in a transport of exaltation as the record of the Baptism and the Temptation leads us to surmise.   What
touchstones for life must have dwelt in His soul!
No other such clear intelligence has ever lived a
life of such imperturbable confidence.   And how like
full tide does He move among men in this fixed,
fundamental mood, without hesitation and without
solicitude, without affectation and without reflection, without self-complacency and without self-
reproach.   With calmness He sat in judgment on
the sacred treasures of the past, and took His station even above Moses, supplementing, denying, out-
reaching him.   In this major mood, He knows that
His appearance determines once and for all the welfare and the ruin of mankind; and in deep affliction
but in clear perspective He discerns in His own rejection the self-rejection of His people.   From this post
of inward calm, He perceives the power of evil
struck to its very heart through His work, feels
empowered to challenge a public judgment of God
upon Himself when He promises to the palsied man
both restoration to health and forgiveness, and casts

His claim in the face of eternity upon an oath which has to do with the final issue of the quarrel between life and death.

Powerful and unshaken, this imperturbable confidence stands back of all His words and deeds, and is impossible to dissociate in the least from them. It is all so extraordinary that none of us even with the utmost effort can think his way into it, and yet it wears such an air of the wholly natural that one cannot possibly think the truth to be otherwise. Whoever has taken full account of this major mood will not be found appealing to the psychiatrist for confirmation of any snap judgment of his own against Jesus, but will recognize that it was His truthfulness and unpretentiousness which impelled Jesus to take this extraordinary name, the Son of God: truthfulness, for it was part of His Commission not to keep to Himself His knowledge of the innermost reality of His nature; for the only thing He could do was to accept it in modesty as the pure gift of God. Calm and luminous as the day, therefore, His imperturbable confidence lights up the World. It all appears so clear and matter of fact that we cease to be aware of any element of incredibility. This degree of confidence is superhuman, and yet its subject lived in a definite, historical situation and was possessed of an individualized spiritual-intellectual endowment.

Let us, then, stand unwaveringly by this fresh impression of reality. Unhampered by any theology and philosophy whatsoever, let us stick to what we see. The riddle of this man shall remain a riddle for us—it shall not with our consent be deprived of its immediate fascination and its immediate effect by the development of a doctrine. Here is a humanity which is diaphanous to the Spirit and to God. Here or nowhere we may catch a presentiment of what happens when God finds full entrance into human actuality and man finds full entrance into divine truth. Here or nowhere we feel is the prime example of how Divine Being can stream through a human being, how a human being may be set aglow by the Divine.

PART III
THE MESSAGE

PART III

THE MESSAGE

OLD-TIME writers addressed themselves at once to the tasks connected with determining the "doctrine" which Jesus preached. Consequently His teaching would be proclaimed not original enough and modern enough to suit them. They would point out that various of its elements had been uttered by His predecessors, and that others had since become obsolete for them as modern men. In their opinion the New Testament records were not reliable enough: Jesus had not spoken systematically; plan and cohesion were lacking, as well as the ability to anticipate the needs of future generations. It was easy, they thought, to show that His was an antiquated world long out of date.

But all that is beside the point if Jesus be considered not as a preacher of a doctrine but as a new locus of emergence for reality, a new mode of life incarnate. Then at once His manner of speech is felt to correspond to this new reality, a speech which does not explain it as a doctrine seeks to do, but illuminates it as a life tries to do—from within; the modest records become satisfactorily informative, and their reluctance to mix comment or to add embellishments wholly admirable. The whole contro-

versy, ever old yet ever new, is silenced by this sin
gle and vital fresh issue.

The new reality which finds its seat in Jesus
appears before us in a garment which has a beauty
all its own. Before asking, What did Jesus say? let
us ask, How did He say it? And the answer is: In
the freest and most individual manner does His soul
become audible to us. No hint is given of any delib-
erations on His part over the words of the Bible, or
of debate over the interpretations of them by others;
His concern is all with the life lived around Him as
it directly touches His mind, which responds to it
with a note from its depths just as it could not help
responding—differing each time according to the
variation in the point of contact and yet always the
same in caliber. Never do intellect, feeling, and will
exhaust the content of His words. Ever rings out
clear an intonation of His soul, intelligible to the
most simple-minded, and yet too profound for those
most richly endowed, far beyond all and yet wholly
strange to none. Full of humanity is His speech in
respect to its imagery, asides, and references, and yet
it comes to the birth pure and free and out of the
depths of an eternally unique Mind. Even where
the form of expression is perfect, it never impresses
us as forced, but rather as the gift of an inspired
moment. Many a parable may have taken a long
time to ripen in the soul of Jesus, but when given to
us it is as ripe fruit from the tree and not as an
artfully prepared dish. Whoever has retained un-
spoiled his sense for things spiritual will take joy
without end in these parables. One breathes in them

.n atmosphere reminiscent of the first day of creation. Not all of them, as they stand in our records, but many—the parables of the Prodigal Son, of the Good Samaritan, of the Sower of the Seed—are like primeval revelations of the soul garmented in words that qualify them to circulate freely and self-reliantly among men.

Tolstoi, the poet, had his reasons ready for assigning to the parables first place in the literature of the world. Not a stroke is wanting and not one is superfluous, and every stroke is sure. Breadth and conciseness, picturesqueness and strength, truth to life and greatness of soul, all wonderfully combine. Everything in these parables is alive; they are steeped in the inner life of Jesus. An attitude of cheerful openness to life that is less hampered and more unrestrained than appears in these parables can hardly be imagined. The most everyday things of life receive friendly attention; easily and naturally they are intertwined with His greatest thoughts of God. In fascinating concord everyday life and the life of eternity are wedded. Salt and bread and leaven, light and candlesticks, raiment and the farthing, house and field, the humblest things which other preachers often hardly venture to mention pass through the gate of observation into the soul of Jesus, and when they come forth again they are clothed in the light of heaven. The naturalness with which Jesus oscillates between the simplest things and the thoughts of eternity could hardly be more self-evident. But does naturalness really fully account for it? Here is rather a heart which despite

the immense demands that it makes upon itself in
behalf of the claims for God is so rich in love that it
can out of its inexhaustible treasure bestow again
and again a transfiguring touch upon the smallest
things. The flame of God in Him intent upon
remolding the world burns so quietly that even the
most insignificant things can creep up close and
borrow of its splendor. All that lives and moves
seems to gather to itself illumination from Jesus—
but then everything seems, at the same time, to have
some contribution to make to Him. Jesus has not
only imparted something of His life to earthly
things, but earthly things have also given a share in
their lot to Him.

Not only was He open to life, but He took joy
in what life opened to Him. Anyone who is suscep-
tible at times has a mood come over him as if suddenly a warm heart could be felt beating within one
of his common ordinary observations. How heartily
Jesus rejoices with the woman over her recovery of
the lost penny. The artless lack of hesitation with
which Jesus moves joyously through life is recog-
nizable in the easy, matter-of-course way He could
let a flash of humor play around a most sublime
mood. Even in the midst of the most pointedly
earnest counsel He can find room for a smile. His
description of the rich farmer is so graphic that we
can fairly see him folding his hands across his
paunch and hear him say: "Have rest now, dear soul,
eat, drink, and be of good cheer." The same thing
is true of the incident of the unjust judge who finally
makes up his mind to help a poor widow, "that she

night not come some day and fly into his face." In
His comparison of His hearers to guests invited to
the table of the King who would rather look over
their newly bought oxen, note the touch of irony in
the "I beg you, pray, excuse me." Never, however,
does His openness of mind to what is going on in the
world make us the least bit uncertain that the
affairs in which His mind is truly engrossed are those
of a higher world. Even when Jesus seems to be
absorbed in the description of our ordinary human
world, one always feels the high world of God at
its back. And, at times, as at the end of His parables, there shoots forth from this higher world with
the weight of a thunderbolt such a blow as this:
"Thou fool, this night thy soul shall be required of
thee: then whose shall those things be which thou
hast accumulated?" Sometimes, however, the
touch is lighter and the words like notes dancing in
the rays of the sun: "some fell on good ground and
sprang up, and bore fruit an hundredfold"; "immediately he putteth in the sickle, because the harvest
is come"; "he went forth for joy and sold all that
he had"; "is thine eye evil with criticism, because
I am so mercifully good?"

We know something of the peculiarities of spirit
and style possessed by the Gospel writers. Of how
they came to preserve these finer touches, we know
little. But still less do we know where else they
could have derived them except from Jesus. Often
an account is so worded as to seem like a delicately
woven veil which scarcely conceals an impressive
joy that grips us deeply. The parable of the Prod-

igal Son is so told that all the depths of love seen.
eager to break through the narrative into the open
Again, the overt ones in the parable of the Good
Samaritan are so wonderful that, though few listen
to them, no one who does will ever forget them.
This is the way, also, to catch the significance of
these parables and stories. That is how we begin
to discover that there is no doctrine to be learned by
us, but a reality which beckons to us to make its
acquaintance. While we think we are simply lis-
tening to an everyday story the sunshine of a higher
world is creeping into our souls. While our minds
are still occupied with these pictures of life which
they contain, suddenly we sense the fact that our
hearts have been vigorously awakened by an inflow
from a much higher life. In the parables the divine
world of Jesus makes its first shy approaches to us
and asks whether we recognize it and are ready to
give it welcome. This point of view renders com-
prehensible to us also that fearsome utterance: "I
speak in parables that they with seeing eyes may
not see and they with hearing ears may not hear."
Does not this saying hang like a gray cloud over
the sunny world of the parables and cast its gloom
over all the life we are thus told we may be missing?
Jesus quotes here the word of an old prophet which
voices the insight of the speaker into the futility of
hoping to communicate heavenly things in the only
language understood by the wholly earthly-minded.
He expresses nothing but a law of life, hard but
true, tragic and yet beneficent in the end. According to that law we perceive nothing of all the stages

·f reality above us save those things to which our
.onging and our striving prepare us to respond. The
parables can bring to the light of day only what
lives deeply hidden in any particular soul—or expose
its poverty. Otherwise, no higher degree of life will,
may, or can be heard at all. Without eyes vision
is impossible and light is of no avail. Jesus was no
formal teacher, but the beacon to new altitudes of
reality.

The other characteristic of the speech of Jesus,
a predilection for strong, overstrong words and
phrases, is explained by exigencies of its own nature.
"And unto him that smiteth thee on the right cheek
offer also the other." How much misunderstanding
has been heaped upon this saying by friend and
enemy alike. Such words of Jesus are not edicts,
they are peans of joy. They do not enunciate laws,
but seek to impart secrets of a higher reality than
can be expressed in common speech. A kind of life
which is new has to create its own language and
has to make that language hyper-emphatic in order
that its message may not be misunderstood or belit-
tled—in this case by those who consider it the height
of wisdom for a man to let his enemy set the tune
to which his inward life shall dance. Jesus is rejoicing that a man can be so free from all feelings of
revenge and spite that no evil done to him in person
will be able to extort a response in kind inside him
of ill will; so free that the effect of continued evi-
dences of hostility will be to bring his inner moral
superiority into play all the more surprisingly and
overwhelmingly. Shall we undertake to fulfill this

word literally? Why not, if the spirit it contains
is thereby expressible? But let us not haggle over
the matter of success or failure in its literal practice. The demand is that the acquaintance of this
new spirit be formed and its wisdom recognized, and
not that the letter be fulfilled. Thus and not otherwise has Jesus interpreted this word by His own
behavior. But He had to express Himself in this
vigorous manner if the full reality which He bore in
Himself were to find untrammeled outlet. To give
free right of way to the tumultuous eruptions of His
inner life, He had to speak so vehemently that His
words glared above the heads of His hearers like
torches and fire beacons of a new world. It was His
destiny, a sublime and impressive lot, that He could
communicate with others only in signals of this
kind. He was not a dealer in doctrine but a new
star in the human firmament, the seat of a disturbingly novel phase of Reality.

What was this novelty? "Repent ye: for the
kingdom of heaven is at hand" points the way to
the answer. Change your whole manner of thinking
and base it hereafter on the principle that the
dominion of God is here! This was the Gospel of
Jesus. All of its single items were derivations of
this one major principle. Everything He said was
truly and most consistently linked to this primary
fiat.

Dominion of God—what did Jesus intend to
cover by this phrase? Did He Himself not take the
common view of his day that this dominion of God
was a new world which would be forcibly imposed

y miracle from above? Was not an annihilating
judgment upon the godless to precede its advent?
Would not a life of earthly joys follow under the
rule of any new dispensation in which even such a
sensuous thing as drinking of the fruit of the vine
would never fail? Are we not told that, in the
presence of His inevitable end, Jesus professed to
know that He Himself would return upon the clouds
of Heaven? And that the great overthrow of the
contemporary world was near, quite near? Surely,
at any rate, His outlook differed wholly from the
shape that was given it by the later interpreters,
differed radically also from the manner in vogue
to-day. It was far more precipitate, tense, circum-
scribed, and direful.

This or that embarrassing word of Jesus has put
some of those who have revered Him into a predica-
ment from which they have attempted to extricate
themselves by interpretations which must be credited to their veneration for Him and not to dishon-
esty. But certain utterances of Jesus, such as these:
"Verily I say unto you, This generation shall not
pass, till all these things be fulfilled"; "Ye shall not
have passed through the cities of Israel, till the Son
of Man be come," will, in the long run, resist every
other interpretation than the nearest and natural
one that Jesus here predicts that which has not been
fulfilled. How does this admission, then, affect our
opinions about Him? About His spirit? About His
character?

Here, again, the answer is that Jesus was not a
teacher, but the seat of a disturbingly novel phase

of reality. The world of ideas in which He lived was
altogether the world of ideas common to His time
He thought the world, among other things, was the
den of a horde of demons whose ruler was Satan.
His thought looked not to a slow evolution of all
things, but to a catastrophic revolution descending
from above. His mind dealt with a great judgment
day bearing a calendar date and the imminence of
a final crisis and winnowing. If Jesus had not lived
in this same world of ideas as His contemporaries,
He would not, indeed, have lived in their world at
all. And if He had lived the life of a foreigner to
their world of ideas, He would not have been able to
touch and affect them—would not have been able,
through them, to affect us. Whoever has something
to proclaim must put it into a form intelligible to
the audience addressed, which means the use of their
language, even their conceptual language. If Jesus
had used the ideology of to-day—as so many objec-
tors we know have desired—to what extent would
He be escaping from the use of the imagery of a
transient world and finding a timeless form for His
news of eternal things? Precisely the ideology of His
time, however, was an incomparably appropriate
container for the inner world of Jesus, because the
task of detaching His inner world from that network can be performed perfectly. After this divi-
sion, how may this inner world and reality that
remains be described?

Jesus felt God to be awesomely present in the core
of His being. God's will performed the offices which
in any other human heart are performed by the

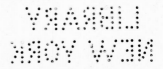

ɔwner's own will. God's way, God's power it was,
which touched the world through Him, His soul was
only its willing vehicle. God's presence lived and
walked the earth in His person, a consummation
incomprehensibly high and indescribably joyful.
God was here. The hour had come when the God
whom the fathers had revered from afar was really
near and close by, only still more inwardly holy; the
God for whom the people had longed, only kinder
in an amazing degree. And this holier, kinder God
was at work, indeed, in Jesus upon the hearts of
men with all the wonderful intensity of His nearness. He was, indeed, moving powerfully in Jesus
down upon the erring world. "Blessed are your eyes,
for they see: and your ears, for they hear. For verily I say unto you that many prophets and righteous
men have desired to see those things which ye see,
and have not seen them; and to hear those things
which ye hear, and have not heard them." With
such imperturbable confidence does the soul of Jesus
abide in this indwelling of God that it is filled with
compassion for all who have not yet experienced
this wonder; and with rejoicing for those who share
the experience. Jesus seems to be looking on like
a spectator and to be speaking like a reporter in
announcing that God really had never before been
so close to earth. "Behold, a greater than Jonah is
here. Behold, a greater than Solomon is here." The
Holy of Holies has chosen the soul of Jesus for its
inner temple; whereas, even the greatest of the
prophets, John the Baptist, must content himself
with serving undeniably as the portico of that

Temple. Surely the ardent desires and the greatest
prophecies of the past never contemplated anything
beyond what had now come to pass, what was
already here: "To-day is this scripture fulfilled in
your ears." Moses himself now steps back into the
assembly of the outgrown. "But, I say unto you."
God was here, unmistakably here and inexpressibly
near—this was something not to be comprehended,
and still less to be disputed. God and mankind had
gotten together at last. How fervid and intrinsi-
cally real their intercourse henceforth was to be, no
one, indeed, could surmise. "No man knoweth the
Son, but the Father; neither knoweth any man the
Father save the Son."

Was there now any other lot at all possible for
men except complete devotion to this program and
its great, great joy? For Jesus, in any case, there
was only one thing possible: complete absorption in
this great experience. And the people? If only,
alas, they might receive their sight! "If thou hadst
known, even thou, at least in this thy day, the
things which belong unto thy peace! But now
they are hid from thine eyes." This people stood
before the choice of its fate; world history before
its crucial turning point.

This imperturbable confidence of Jesus, intense
enough to make the people almost recoil from Him,
beams clear and strong throughout everything which
the Gospels relate to us. The new phase of reality
emerging there had to seize upon extraordinary
language by which to utter itself. When Jesus
struggled to achieve an understanding of Himself

nd sought ways and means to express that understanding to others, what words from the store then available could offer themselves to Him more naturally than the imposing terms Messiah and Kingdom of God? Within the shell provided by these terms the new phase of reality grew; it is from the hulls that seeds of corn obtain their first growth. Such a hull supplies protection, but may also do harm by barring out too much—it may conserve and it may retard growth. What harvest lies in the hull depends upon the nature of the seed and how victorious it will be in bursting through. The expectation of the fast-approaching dissolution of the world, for instance, did Jesus great service: it saved Him from embroilment in matters of State and thus from becoming a politician; it prevented Him from specializing in intellectual questions and thus from becoming a dogmatist; it prevented Him from drawing up a program for the regulating of life in its details and thus from becoming a person in practical affairs. Everything will be quite changed, will become completely new very soon now when the domination of God breaks in upon the world and takes command. So the expectation that the end of the world was near exerted an unheard-of, powerful pressure to hold Him firm to His great work. The hull protects the kernel. But the hull did not carry shielding to the point of doing any real damage to the seed. All these extraordinary expectations did not, if we look closely, effect in Jesus any alteration of His moral ideas, any falsification of moral purposes, but rather reënforced His moral feelings. "Be

not excited, but be prepared!   Be not drunk with
longing for the future, but be faithful to your present post.   Live not in idle waiting, but in hard
labor.   Strive not for the unusual, but fulfill the
nearest obligation, and give joy to thy neighbor."
"Inasmuch as ye have done it unto one of the least
of these my brethren, ye have done it unto me."
This was the way Jesus taught His disciples to prepare to meet the end of the world.   The kernel
struggled its way to victorious germination through
the hull; not, to be sure, without great resistance
from the environment in which that kernel lay
nestled.   How hard Jesus had to battle for a foot-
hold for His program against the superficial programs
of watchful waiting and guerrilla warfare then in
vogue!   And yet His program was not overwhelmed
by these others.   How freely and certainly the new
phase of reality emerging in Jesus almost loosens
itself from the world of popular Jewish thought in
which it became entangled!

The Dominion of God ready to begin operations
—without waiting for any warfare of worlds or men!
This was, then, the reality which Jesus felt in fer-
ment in Himself; this was the new order of things
which He saw at work in the preliminaries.   Man
gladly ruled by God, God with free right of way in
men—the joy of it He experienced in Himself, this
He yearned for others to realize.   Who is this God
of Jesus?   For us the answer is not to be found by
examining all sorts of statements about God, but
through insight into the inner world in which Jesus
lived.   Jesus knew His being was geared to a power

that was above all powers, whose mandate nothing in all the world could withstand. If God is unwilling, neither sparrow can fall from the roof nor high priest pronounce sentence of death. Evil powers might be at work, but God's power can withstand and conquer them whenever He wills. Whether it be a prayer that seems to go unheard or the redemption of all men that is being postponed, it is due to no want of power, but always to some decision to withhold its exercise. God's will and nothing else is at the bottom of everything that happens.

An exceedingly noble attitude toward life, it is clear, thus becomes feasible for man. It assures him God's familiar company even when weighty temptations or the hostility of his fellow men make a man feel isolated. Under all contingencies he is assured God speaks with him; through everything God can be depended upon to be near. Thus events and circumstances, immediate and remote, are resolved into spirit, which can be perceived by the spirit of man, into the Spirit of God, which longs to be welcomed gladly in this way by the soul of man. The ideas of Jesus concerning the creation and government of the world may have been different from our own, but that the fact that His life knew itself to be wholly encompassed and fenced about by the omnipotence of God's Spirit is substantially real stands unimpaired by this difference.

For Jesus God, who is pure spirit and power above all powers, is good—good through and through. In Him there is not save the will for the good. "Be ye therefore perfect, even as your Father which is in

Heaven is perfect." In God's presence nothing of
evil can escape condemnation, even though it hide
in the most hidden recesses of the soul: "Whosoever
is angry with his brother . . . shall be in danger of
judgment." Face to face with the purity of God
everything else appears to be stained: "No one is
good but God alone." Only single, undivided good
will can do work to suit Him: "You cannot serve
God and Mammon." The holy purity of good will
like unto that of God which lived in the heart of
Jesus possessed a dazzling luminousness. Exposed
to its illumination the best in the soul of man stirs
into life, and whatever evil is present there is inex-
orably disclosed. Jesus seems to be standing before
God, suffused in light without a shadow. Ringed
about entirely by evil, venomously attacked by evil,
inescapably caught in a vice of evil, Jesus has no
eyes, nevertheless, for aught else than the pure Will
of God as it lies exposed to His gaze turned within,
for to Him it is the only real power of the Universe.
This was the wonderful mode of reality in which He
dwelt.

But this God, who is good through and through,
is also kind through and through, is kindness itself.
The way Jesus speaks of God makes a really warm
human appeal. God gives unceasingly and discrim-
inates against none; He forgives without reservation
and without reproof; gives good gifts without end.
He rejoices deeply over every spark of good, wherever it appears. He advances without hesitation to
meet any heart making advances toward Him. God
is in unflagging pursuit of any life which goes astray

from Him. The appellation "Father" fell from the lips of Jesus with an accent of profound kindness, which those who have heard it once cannot forget, but cherish ever after as the most holy experience of their lives. "Father"—life itself seems on the point of opening up in order to put us into contact with a mystery of endless depth and indescribable happiness! "Father"—as if the soul of the world's history would make itself known, and compel us to say, Behold! we all do live within the embrace of a great and fundamentally good heart, which feels nothing but love for its children! With joy of a depth and of intrinsic tenderness whose high appeal goes to the heart, do the eyes of Jesus rest upon the Father. It is the Father who cannot forget his lost son but keeps waiting and looking for his return; who does not make the son come to meet him first but hurries to greet his son; who does not force the son to ask to be taken back but embraces him with joy; who does not humiliate him with reproaches but honors him highly, asking no questions nor blaming him, but almost heaping a love upon him that is greater than of old. This is a father who can, without any hesitation, display pure joy and kindness at the first indication of genuine repentance of his son.

Nobody can truly say of Jesus that He was unacquainted with the gloomy and wretched sides of life. His news about this Father lights up through the centuries His own last night of inward tumult and a malefactor's death. In that hardest hour did this appellation "Father" confirm its reality to Him.

Jesus imagined no world of dreams to be around
Him in which to hide away from the truth, but He
simply read the nature of God from the book of this
humdrum world with that fresh sense for reality
which He never lost.

The Father who makes his sun to rise upon the
evil and upon the good, who clothes the flowers of
the field so splendidly that the splendor of Solomon
is made to seem poor beside them, who causes the
seed to spring up while the sower rests in slumber
now that he can do nothing more—this Father
makes Himself known to Jesus, without any medita-
tion, as Spirit to Spirit.   But Jesus also reads in
the soul of man tidings of the nature of God.   The
best and the noblest that lives in a human heart
becomes transparent to his gaze, which also looks
through past these into the depths of God.   "If ye
then, being evil, know how to give good gifts unto
your children, how much more shall your Father
which is in Heaven give good things to them that
ask him?"   If, then, the shepherd rejoices over a
single lamb that was lost, how much more "shall
joy be in heaven over one sinner that repenteth than
over ninety and nine just persons which need no
repentance."

The soul creates for itself a God after its own
image, it is true, but only because it has learned to
know itself to be created in the image of God.   Not
as a supernatural form of knowing but as a vision
which penetrates through the facts of nature to a
"knowledge of God," do the words of Jesus about the
God of kindness pass themselves on to us.   He

knows that a kingdom of kindness—an unfathomable, unconquerable kindness—buoys up and holds together the dark kingdom of the earth. This does not mean that He is blind to the misery and evil but that He sees through the misery and evil, and when He does He sees the father in the background. In untroubled, full human contact He lives in our world of actuality, but with unswerving positiveness He is aware that pure love—the most holy kindness of the Spirit of God—is the true reality back of the world.

His program was to invest this Spirit of God with power over men. The whole message of Jesus can be summed up in a single sentence: Jesus of all men was the only one who has taken God really altogether seriously. Man is to take God seriously with His entire nature and life—this is the final and deepest meaning of His message, just as it was the final and deepest content of His own life. Putting aside all popular expectations and eliminating all external factors, the Dominion of God, in the sense which Jesus meant, is nothing other than the revolutionary idea that God should come into His own among men. Everything else branches out and is an elaboration from this active principle which makes itself felt with weight everywhere: God alone is all in all! "If one believes at all, then one must believe wholly otherwise than one does usually believe"—these words of Nietzsche hit upon the meaning of the active principle of Jesus' faith.

Wholly true unto the innermost and wholly resolute unto the extreme exacted of it must the service be which is devoted to God. Wholly true unto the innermost: every kind of service of God, doing good, prayer, sacrifice, must be performed with absolute purity of intent for the sake of God Himself. That glory would suffer impairment were any inferior motive admitted into our devotions, such as the desire to receive recognition from men; any lesser thought, like the comparison of ourselves with others; or any slightest complaisant feeling, such as letting the left hand know what the right hand does. All such slights stain the honor of God, which should be the sole consideration in our hearts and alone rule them whenever we come to Him. Not only religious communion with God, but the moral service of God cannot ever at all be thought of too scrupulously. Our deeds, our opinions, and our most secret desires belong to God. Even a glance violates the seventh commandment. No superfluous verbiage must profane the presence of God. No implacable thought shall be harbored in the heart. Jesus supersedes the old views about what is pure and impure in a single great saying, and does it easily and naturally: "Do ye not perceive that whatsoever thing from without entereth into the man, it cannot defile him. . . . That which cometh out of the man, that defileth the man."

Wholly true unto the innermost! And wholly resolute in fidelity to the extreme of what is exacted. The parables of the treasure in the field and of the pearl of great price acquire incomparable charm from the fact that they pour a mood of a great happiness over those unheard-of demands, which makes them

ppear self-evident, natural, and full of joy. "And
or joy thereof goeth and selleth all that he hath,
and buyeth that field." If the pure pearl of great
price is really worth more, then no action is more
natural. The ethic of heroism is changed here into
an ethic of nature, into a plain and effective law of
life which turns it into a joy. But this resoluteness
in devotion to the service of God pertains not only
to the things of the world, but also to the things of
self. To relinquish everything, to deny one's own
self, such a spirit does this resolute fidelity demand.
"And if thy right eye offend thee, pluck it out, and
cast it from thee"; "and if thy right hand offend
thee, cut it off, and cast it from thee." Nothing
could be more precious to us than our eye, and the
hand is the most necessary to life of the members
of the body. Jesus has spoken here with such
unparalleled clearness and power, that we would
think He had cast about for a form of statement
which should not be forgotten nor go unheard
through the centuries. Are harder demands possible than these of Jesus? Yet, are there demands
any plainer or more obvious? Is it not self-evident
that a man would rather lose his eye than his life?
Does it not go without saying that a man would
give up himself to get hold of God? How could
anyone think otherwise even for a moment, or act
otherwise, who takes God seriously enough?

The God of holiness in its purity is to be taken
absorbingly, in all earnest; but the God of great
kindness is to be taken no less absorbingly. Any
fear of fate or the future is to be banished from

one's thought, even from the innermost ground of the soul. Also in this Jesus speaks a word which could not be plainer nor more popular: "But the very hairs of your head are all numbered." In such sayings we feel deeply even to-day how intense was the inner struggle of Jesus to win over the souls of men. With a bold, masterful stroke He takes from men the last battle ground on which their mistrust could still maintain itself. Never, indeed, has any man worried enough about his safety or future to count all the hairs of his head that he might take note that not a single one was missing. But this is precisely what needs to be hammered into the heads of men: God's care embraces not only the great human necessities but the small, even the smallest, about which you yourself do not think at all! A hair falls from the head silently and unobserved—nothing more insignificant happens in our whole life. So nothing of less concern could Jesus have selected to set before the souls of men, for all time, the all-inclusiveness of divine oversight and the unreasonableness of human anxiety.

That men should not work was not what Jesus meant to say. What He had in view was anxiety, depression, and fear for the future which rob us of the hours so spent, weaken our spirit, debase our soul, and frustrate our whole life. In order to banish anxiety, root and branch, Jesus summons the birds of the air as heralds of divine kindness, and the flowers of the field, and there runs through his words a hearty joy, a divine happiness as though the world were disclosing its glory for the first time,

s though all the clouds over human life were being
driven away forever and a serene sky would arch
itself over men eternally.   We never feel more
intensely convinced than we do here just what kind
of life Jesus wishes His disciples to share.   He
thought too highly of the soul to permit it to waste
its energy in anxiety.   The soundness of this principle cannot be questioned, namely, the soul cannot
come at all to the adoption of a perfect resolution
to take sides with God without a perfect trust in
God.   Trust in God, body and life, for time and
eternity, is impossible unless every last suspicion
about the wholly personal, friendly good will of
God is banished from the innermost recesses of the
heart.

But even this exalting trust in God did not deter
Jesus from calling men to the most insistent use of
prayer.   God knows beforehand all that we need and
ask for; God needs not to be prompted by, to say
nothing of wheedled by, many words, and yet He
wants to be sought in prayer; God can be won in
prayer.   Such happy, assured familiarity does Jesus
use in speaking of speech with God that He is bold
enough to compare Him with a judge who will permit himself to be wearied by persistence, and a
friend who can be won over by importunity.   The
God thus spoken of by Jesus is one and the same
with the God whose purity permeates Him deeply,
and His object is to fill men with a wholly unafraid
confidence in God which shall be always sure that
"every one that asketh, receiveth; and he that seek-
eth findeth; and to him that knocketh it shall be

opened." The words Jesus uses here are plain; bu.
they also need to be supplemented and expounded
through what He did. What extraordinary experiences were responsible for this victorious confidence in God? What had He wrested for Himself
from God by insistent seeking? Since even Jesus
in Gethsemane won nothing requested for Himself
from God by persistent prayer, since His personal
wants were so unpretentious and He was so reserved
in His public deeds, the amazing experiences upon
which His recommendation of prayer is based must
have occurred only in the sphere of His inner life,
and it is gripping reminiscences of these experiences
which resound in these counsels. It is, then, in His
inner life that He knew, better than our lukewarm
generation knows, that all that is highest has to be
stormed and conquered by a power of insistence such
as most people do not even suspect exists. He certainly did not wish to advise us to importune God
for the fulfillment of capricious desires, but He did
keenly urge us to come to God with our souls all
aglow if we expect to take internal possession of
God and His gifts. It will not avail to squeeze the
last drop of dictionary sense from the words of
Jesus. What is needed is that we should evaluate
rightly the reality which emerged in Him, in the
form of an elemental, heaven-storming confidence in
God which expects all from God and which gives
itself completely up to God.

But the highest that can be said of Him remains
yet unspoken. All that precedes—unconditioned
fidelity to His decision to side with God, unconquer-

able trust in Him—is only the open road beyond which a most splendid goal looms visible on the horizon: resemblance to God, union with God. Jesus has said things in this connection which sound overarrogant, words which we would not tolerate from the lips of anyone else: "Be ye therefore perfect, even as your Father which is in heaven is perfect." That old fateful word from the Garden of Eden story, "Ye shall be as God!" is here seriously proclaimed, is accepted calmly and freely as true, and in its deepest and purest sense is set up as the goal of mankind. A greater than this has never been attributed to man, nor has a greater ever been expected of man.

This is truly the view beyond compare of the Dominion of God. "If there were gods, how could I endure it not to be a god!" Whatever these words of Nietzsche, for all their overassertiveness, contain of the noblest longing of man, the clear saying of Jesus just quoted is the answer to this, as the day is the answer to the morning mist. And this saying of Jesus marks the moment in the world history of the discovery of the North Pole of the highest nobility of mankind. A higher summit of salvation and of sublimity cannot be set before men—to be God-like! And this discovery was announced by one to whom of all who have walked the earth the nature of God became most luminous. "Be ye therefore perfect, even as your Father which is in heaven is perfect." It is not, we repeat, a command, but the simple reflection of an inner reality in Him conveying the wonderful certainty that the way into the

depth of the divine nature is wholly free and open
to genuine human longing and striving, and that
just penetration to these depths is that most sublime
destination kept in store for us by the divine Love.

This culminating, however, is to be no self-com-
placent assemblage of all the virtues, but life out
of God's Life. That most Holy Will, which desires
to see its longing for the highest salvation of the
world accomplished, wills to become the life of our
life. This is the way that perfection and Christian
love are to be understood if the words and life of
Jesus do truly interpret each other. Love is not
a commandment, not even a disposition of the mind
—it is nothing other than the living God in full
action in the heart of man. The disciple of this Love
is not to be absorbed in random, small services of
his own choosing, but in the one great service to
his life in God alone. Jesus Himself did no otherwise. This Love is felt as a fire which is willing
to consume itself if thereby it might fuse the whole
world into the perfected life lived under the sway
and splendor of God.

Jesus in speaking of Love adapted the language
of the preachers of this world's wisdom. "Therefore all things whatsoever ye would that men should
do to you, do ye even so to them"—a slight verbal
modification of the popular adage, what people do
to you, do that to them, but it changes everything.
What you want other people to do to you! Instantly
all our proposed acts toward others cease to feel at
home in the kingdom of retaliation and find their
only congenial resting place to be the kingdom of

he revelation of God. Our deeds are to be no longer
instinctive reactions in kind to the way we are
treated, but are always to be the outcome of the best
we wish from them. Our line of conduct is no
longer a copy suggested to us by the evil which an
enemy wills for us, but a copy suggested always by
the God who wills the good and does the good, both
to friend and enemy.

At this point, let us revert to His saying concerning the right and left cheek. No deed of an enemy
should be able to force something of its own com-
plexion out of us; nor anything less, indeed, than an
attitude in accord with the sublimity of a love which
grows more and more free in expressing itself, more
and more glad. Nietzsche proclaimed with the joy
of a new discovery that true nobility acts according
to the principle! To give to everyone what is mine,
and not to everyone only what is his! Exactly this
is the meaning of the words of Jesus, whom
Nietzsche has despised as weak and slavish. A
spring of living water, overflowing its basin, over-
comes all that gets in its way, and the more obstruc-
tion it meets, the more powerful and more abun-
dant, the more unexpected and more unconquerable,
is its flood. So is the divine Love. Jesus did not
intend to speak enigmatical words, but to make crystal clear deeply sublime paradoxes which the divine
principle of Love all powerful in the world makes
come semi-miraculously true. To place Buddha
above Christ because he taught men to spare their
enemies rather than to love them—an inhuman and
impossible demand in some people's estimation—is

to take up a position far below the spirit of Jesus
How can God meet an enemy otherwise than with
kindness?   Remember, He has nothing else to meet
Him with, and has room in His nature for nothing
else than kindness.   How is it possible to think that
God could be in us and act in us otherwise than He
does elsewhere?   Not to be reconciled means to be
in self-exile from God.   Therefore, it is surely better to forgive the worst, seventy times seven, than
to forego the best.   There lives in us just as much
of the presence of God and of community with God
as there dwells in us of forgiving and conquering
love: "Do ye not know of what Spirit ye are the
children?"   "That ye may be the children of your
Father which is in heaven."

Jesus used also an Old Testament quotation to
explain the meaning of love to His disciples: "Love
thy neighbor as thyself."   This saying contains
nothing exaggerated or excessive.   God is taken seriously, that is all.   We remain faithful if not to the
letter, certainly to the spirit of Jesus, when we say:
Where God, the God of great kindness becomes a
reality in the heart, there one can love himself only
with the love of God, and can love his neighbor as
himself.   "As long as you grant more to yourself
than to that man whom you have never seen, so long
have you never yet for a moment looked into the
heart of God," said Meister Eckhart, a man who
understood the divine life as few have understood it.   This great life of divine love does
not lie behind and below as something outgrown
in the progress of mankind, but is on beyond and

high above anything thus far attained. This life is not "obsolete," but is hardly yet out of the embryo; yea, we have scarcely become acquainted with it in our imagination. He who would live the life in God must also love in company with God, must love in all ways as God loves, even the enemy; he must love even himself in the way God loves him. A delicacy and depth pertain to this love as it is described for us in the parable of the Good Samaritan over which we cannot cease to wonder.

This way of loving as thus exhibited in the full splendor of this life shows itself to be constrained and yet sacrificial, tender and yet unyielding, unpretentious and yet profound, equal to the present hour and yet looking far ahead, quiet and yet assured, firm in deed and yet warm of heart. On this wise the golden law of God as to serving is to be understood, the golden law of service which is the greatest and most splendid "Revolution from above" that men have ever known. It is true that the outgoings of this love find their way first of all to the one who needs help, just as the kindness of God Himself takes to its heart first of all the poor and weak; but the intent of this love is to bring salvation to all the world, for it is something that can go far beyond the immediate help of one's neighbor and ennoble all work and sanctify all life. The spirit of such a love is God in man, is life out of God's life, is the likeness of God in man and coöperation with God in His will to save the world.

Far too much have people forgotten what Jesus was in trying to make out what He thought; they

have forgotten what Jesus brought in trying to hunt
down what He expected was going to happen. Whatever His conceptions of the end of the world may
have been, the Kingdom of God or the Dominion
of God was for Him an inner region of reality to
which mankind simply needed a guide. This Dominion of God is a kingdom which man must strive
for and force his way into; and yet, alone among
all kingdoms, it must be accepted in the end by a
man with the unprejudiced and fully receptive mind
of a child. This Dominion of God, alone, begins
unpretentiously with an individual here and there
and yet will win for itself the whole world. It alone
is present in all the finer forces of God's spirit and
yet must be found by us. "The kingdom of heaven
is like unto treasure hid in a field; the which when
a man hath found, he hideth, and for joy thereof
goeth and selleth all that he hath, and buyeth that
field." The Kingdom of Heaven, Dominion of God
—or whatever Jesus might call it—is not an expectation which must wait upon the future for its
appearance, but a most joyful, present thing only
waiting to be appropriated.

But did Jesus not promise the Kingdom of Heaven
as a recompense? Is His teaching not heavily bur-
dened with the thoughts of reward? Do not His
ethics, just for this reason, stand far below the ethics
of the great Greek teachers? We find it necessary
even to-day to raise questions of this kind. Had
Jesus as a preacher to the common people accommo-
dated His speech to men on various levels, it would
be no occasion for surprise, and we would simply

this reality, as Jesus saw it, He Himself lived up to the requirements of the highest life, and in this reality others have felt the beginnings of the highest life. If Jesus was Life, must He not be the Truth, too?

PART IV
THE SIGNIFICANCE OF JESUS
FOR OUR OWN TIME

PART IV

THE SIGNIFICANCE OF JESUS
FOR OUR OWN TIME

Is it, after all, still necessary to discuss the significance of Jesus for the present age? The world is made up of many very different individuals. Any one into whose hands this little book has happened to come, has probably already discovered whether it can be of service to him in meeting the needs of his life. But the fact that all outstanding significance whatsoever for this age has been contested or denied to Jesus repeatedly and positively does make it necessary to look squarely in the face of all the points which are brought up to-day against Jesus. That will prepare us once again to look into the face of Jesus and ask Him what His challenge is to modern civilization.

In what ways, then, do men deny the significance of Jesus for the present age? The most radical attack upon it declares that Jesus never lived at all. The historical reality of His existence, it is said, will remain at least uncertain and even improbable in the future. Binding proof which will release us from all dispute and doubt will never be possible. We do not intend to overlook the gains with which the movement of recent years against the historical

reality of Christ should be credited, in spite of its
irritating features. It has drawn the attention of
people generally to religious matters. It has raised
new questions of far-reaching importance, destined
to occupy attention for a long time to come, which
certainly have not always been taken seriously
enough. It has concentrated on a decisive issue the
great spiritual struggle over the world-significance
of Christianity, which always tends to fritter itself
away in skirmishes and guerrilla warfare. It has
done us a salutary and valuable service in compelling us to state anew, give more thorough reflection
to, and answer more adequately the fundamental
question of the relation between history and the
eternal world of spirit, between Jesus and the Christ.
The main battle, it is true, will probably be lost by
those who attack the historicity of Jesus. . . .

Our previous discussion has avoided questions of
detail, such as whether Jesus is mentioned in the
only work of a contemporary, Flavius Josephus, on
Jewish history. Even if the passage in question be
a later interpolation, we shall never learn with certainty whether or not a passage of the same general
importance stood where the suspected passage is
now found. Furthermore, even if this supposition,
to judge by the whole context, has to be regarded as
improbable, there are so very many motives which
could have induced a contemporary to be silent
about Jesus—motives historically lost to view—that
this absence of references to Him possesses little or
no significance.

This particular question is one of many of its kind

which might have been raised. And if the sober
experience of historians finds little of value in
descriptions of spiritual experience such as we have
endeavored to give in these pages, these objec-
tors forget that, considering the mass of guesses
which must ever remain questionable, their own
estimates of history can, only too often, scarcely
claim a greater degree of certainty. However, a
single unitary picture of Jesus is the very sort to
exert the strongest effect upon the present controversy, an effect due not to logic but to psychology.
Many of our conclusions in the historical field possess only psychological probability and not logical
certainty. If tokens of historical events which are
of a psychological nature remain embedded in
their naturalness in an historical record, they constitute a witness that the record is not a product of
folklore or of poetic art. When the Italian Vanini
was led out to execution after his condemnation for
blasphemy against God, he is reported, picking up
on the way a blade of straw, to have said: "Had I
no other evidence for the existence of God, this blade
of straw would be enough for me." Single remarks
of Jesus, such as the wonderful announcement: "I
came to send fire on the earth; and what will I, if
it be already kindled? But I have yet a baptism to
be baptized with; and how am I straitened till it be
accomplished"—a single remark of this kind, in our
judgment, overthrows the contention that the figure
of Jesus in the Gospels is a casual product of folklore or a deliberate work of poetic art. Such a record persuades us that we are confronted in it by

an imposing human being fully alive. We admit that our Gospel writers show lack of agility in their thinking, and of style in their writing; but we know, also, that their accounts present a figure unique in its humanity and human in its uniquenes, composed of many quite different individual characteristics, which at the same time preserve so great an inner consistency among themselves that these unusual elements unite to form a convincing, single, unitary picture. The Being we see here embodies a splendor of manhood now for the first time receiving belated recognition, after the centuries have prepared the way by sharpening and schooling our insight into the worth of personality.

Is it not likely that the day will come when people will consider it to be one of the strangest errors of spiritual biography that anyone ever doubted the historical existence of Jesus? Will not posterity be astonished over such want of insight into psychological possibility, even in brilliant scholars? To be sure, the danger is not past that we shall read now and then something into our estimate which was foreign to the historical Jesus. But how much less, we dare maintain, is that other danger past that we shall not discover at all many things which did belong to the historical Jesus? He who would restrict himself to what is unimpeachably certain might well be reminded that in this way he will never find access to the highest realities of life. Books enough have been written upon Jesus for us to know what results from that method which professes to take a coldly scientific view of Jesus—it

is in truth a method soulless and without understanding. This coldly scientific approach is just
the best way to miss the truth of history. It pro-
duces colorless pictures, thin in line, and which correspond the least to reality. Therefore, any individual point which may be deemed improbable and
untenable may be abandoned, and still, we maintain,
a single unitary Figure there speaks out loud so
distinctly for itself that in the long run the reality
of its voice cannot fail to be heard. His authen-
ticity does not depend upon patching together its
four quarters to make a full proof, but rather upon
the fact that an impressive whole can be visible even
if its outlines in certain particulars remain in a state
of uncertainty. Where in all the world has a figure
so luminous, so fully human and superhuman as is
Jesus, ever been produced, either by the imagination of a single artist or the soul of a people?

In the Synoptic Gospels traces may still be seen
of such a picture of Jesus as might have been drawn
by the unstudied folklore type of art, while from the
Gospel of John we may surmise how conscious poetic
art might have depicted Him. But Jesus is no crea-
ture of folklore. He is too true to life, tower though
He does to heaven. His creator—if He were not a
real person—could only have been a poetic artist
of the highest rank, one who could make a success
of the task and at the same time conceal himself.
He would have had to be able to adapt the figure of
his imagination so cleverly to a circle of plain men
that it would seem alive to them and a historical
reality, and also stick in their memories even though

it was far beyond their comprehension. And in addition to all this genius, he would have had to be actuated by an intensely unselfish desire to further the purest salvation of mankind. To take refuge in this alternative is to solve one riddle by putting a lot of others in its place.

There is another quite different angle, also, from which people deny the significance of Jesus for the present age. They say, To be sure, Jesus once lived; but He is alive no longer. The world and its advancing life have long ago gone on their way and left Him behind. It is a sin against the laws of development to chain ourselves to a past time, however significant it may have been. We do ourselves wrong if we cling to a single personality, however great he may have been. Our duty is to take firm hold of the material which experience supplies, to give free and unobstructed outlet to the life which surges up in us. We have kept our eyes on the past long enough. The task now is to give the ship of mankind its head into the future under full sail instead of tethering it by some anchor-rope of the past which gives it leeway only for futile, restless tossings. Therefore, they say, away with history; away with even the greatest names on its roll of honor.

Our reply is that we do not wish at all to anchor the ship of mankind to the past, but to lade it with a full cargo of the treasures of history for use on its future voyaging. The familiar shore line of the ancient world may have to be left behind, but these treasures at least shall go with us. We would not

Jhere to the history of the past in ways that would weaken us, but in those other ways capable of making us wise. A feeling of superiority to past cultures may lead us far astray even in the subjective field of man's inner experiences, and shut us off from the profit that awaits harvesting from the achievements that constitute the heritage of history. That is the very reason we have gone to Jesus and asked: Who are you? What is your significance for us to-day? The present age has not yet established itself on any calm, sound footing with the past, but oscillates between extremes. So let the critics who say Jesus is outgrown by all means try to carry human development beyond the point to which Jesus carried it. The more earnestly and faithfully the attempt is made, the less it will run the risk of going astray through vanity, superficiality, passion for innovation, or hostility against Christianity, and the less humanity will run the risk of losing anything by it. In this way we shall either win a truly higher life than any which has heretofore existed, or achieve a vision of the higher life already lived in Jesus. Either would be a blessing. But hitherto whatever has professed itself to be an advance upon the character and message of Jesus has always really fallen short of them and betrayed a lack of comprehension of Him.

While we do not intend to stand still and let the world leave us behind, we see no possibility of any advance in the direction of surpassing Jesus. Who would not experience the greatest joy at finding an ideal higher than Jesus? Were somebody to assure

us that a finer metal than gold has been found, w
would listen attentively and investigate the matter
thoroughly, but we would not cast away whatever
gold we possessed; we would still be on our guard
against wasting it. But gold can lose value much
more easily than truth can become obsolete. It is
a mistake to suppose that the world progresses from
one truth to another. As the eternal Spirit is a
unit, so also is truth. It discloses itself gradually,
but never changes its essence. Once true, always
true. Even the truths of Hellenism and of Hinduism
have neither perished nor become obsolete. Truths
only retire at times into the background, or they
appear in new garments, or become components in
higher syntheses of truths. But in the basal relation of the human spirit to the riddle of the universe, the same fundamental attitudes recur continually. Why may not the most comprehensive of
these attitudes have been embodied in Jesus once
for all time, to serve permanently as a type of what
is best, truest, and most humanly fruitful?

But, it is to be remembered, Jesus was a Semite,
a man of great genius, but a Jew and nothing else!
Is it not a fact that our thought and feeling of every
people are so thoroughly dominated by race that
we ought to keep ourselves free from infection by
foreign elements and turn away from Jesus, if we
wish to remain true to our Aryan lineage, and be
sure that we do not play false to our race?

Is it necessary, then, to prove that Jesus was an
Aryan before we can take anything without mis-
givings from Him? In our judgment foreignness of

race seems less dangerous to our intellectual integrity than the fear of what is alien.

Who would deprive himself of the wealth of stimulus which comes from the intellectual experience of Spinoza by saying to himself, but this man was a Jew? What is fair toward Spinoza is certainly right to concede to Jesus. Just because we *are* Aryans we should be emancipated enough to weigh everything with an open mind, and sturdy enough to assimilate and make it our own. Just because we *are* Aryans we should be unwilling to raise a bar against anybody by questioning his race. And if the old doubting query, "What good can come out of Nazareth," is put to us, a query which has now attained to world significance, we are still content with the old answer, "Come and see."

Again, from still another side do people deny the significance of Jesus for the present age. They ask, Can anything past and gone any longer possess decisive significance for faith? Surely the business of religion is to deal with our present relation to the mystery of existence, that is, to God! Does that not mean that we paralyze the vital nerve of faith if we try to approach God only by way of the detour of history? In line with this point of view, it is said, "Those who hold anything historical to be an indispensable basis for faith have no true idea at all of what faith really means."

Moreover, the opposition to any significance of Jesus for this age becomes yet sharper. Is the truth of the record handed down to us by history ever more than a probability? Does not all history, by

its very nature, consist only of sums of probabilities?
It will never be possible for anyone to prove to us
incontestably that Luther ever lived. Granted a
high, or even the highest degree of probability to the
conclusion that Jesus once lived, that probability
remains a probability, while faith lives on certainty.
If the debates of recent years had been able to show
only this one thing, namely, that no one can prove
the historical reality of Jesus with infallible certainty, would this alone not be deadly fatal, in the
long run, to the Christian faith as it has been held
valid through all the centuries?

Let us grant now the most extreme concession, and
suppose that someone supplies incontestable proof
that Jesus never lived, that the portrait in the Gospels is after all a fiction, slowly elaborated in the
course of time—what then? We would have to
unlearn much, possibly with pain, and assuredly
with great difficulty. But if we take all those who
have, through this New Testament Jesus, arrived
at the conviction that behind the appearances of
this world God lives and rules and has good and
great things in store for us far beyond the bounds of
this life, that He wills to exalt us into fellowship
with Him and to renew us through His Spirit—if
we take all these people and ask them whether the
loss of the historical Jesus has entailed the loss of
these certainties at one stroke, not one of them would
answer Yes. But if anyone did answer Yes, he
would demonstrate thereby that the truth of Jesus
had never been put to the proof in his life. After
all, every true believer accepts what Jesus has said,

ot because Jesus said it, but because it is true. We heed the words of Jesus not on the score of His authentication to us as the one sent by God; on the contrary, we do hold Him to be the one sent of God because His sayings have verified themselves in our heart and life.

Could we then get along without Jesus altogether? Could we, perhaps, dispense with Him and find all the truth of which we stand in need in other sources? However that question might be answered, the fact remains incontestable that the truth of God has come to us in just this way through Jesus. If we could no longer rest in the belief that God has thus spoken to us through this single man, we would then have to suppose that He has spoken to us through a whole course of human history pervaded by the Spirit of God. And we would then have to admit that all the things taught in this larger history will be found to be embodied, in the last analysis, in an ideal figure of light named Jesus, which is alive for us in the New Testament. The things which the Jesus of the Gospels teaches and lives prove themselves to be true in our experience. Who this Jesus was—whether a living man or an inspired fiction—is an important, but not the most important question. We do not wish to keep repeating how entirely improbably the assertion seems to us that Jesus never lived. But thousands of men to-day would feel it a deeply essential benefit to be relieved inwardly from all the uncertainty naturally attendant upon a faith based on authority. They wish to assume a free, worthy attitude toward things his-

torical, and at the same time be able to take also
a new, calm joy in Jesus, which is far from all anxiety over the possibility of unexpected attacks and
surprises from science.

Is not this equivalent, after all, to binding faith
in chains to history, and refusing to allow it its freedom to develop in the present up to its full capacity
according to its own nature? To which we reply,
How preposterous it is to tear history and the present apart in this way. What, then, is the present?
What would be left were all history taken away
from the present? Actually no moment of our life
is like what it would be, were we the first men in
the world; we experience everything as men whose
past is contained, and is still alive in their present;
and, therefore, by reason of this past that is alive
in our present, the past of humanity is alive. In a
vacuum present, destitute of historical antecedents,
nothing at all could be experienced. Apart from
the present, certainly history ceases to be alive;
but, also, apart from history, certainly no present
can manage to exist.

In answer, then, to the question asked above, we
would now express the conviction that those who
hold that faith, cut off from its own feeders in history, is able to preserve its vitality, lack any comprehension of the nature of life. Applying this principle to ourselves, we may say that we draw life
from that divinely great chapter of history which
has to do with Jesus. This history affords nurture
to us in accord with our individual nature and continues to develop itself in us as our nature gives it

ay. But without these feeders of history to draw
pon, we would be religiously blind and poor. The
spirit of God would not awake to its full activity
within us unless the call of God came to it from
outside; and He does call us in some way through
the chapter of history which is associated with the
name of Jesus, even if this chapter does embrace
only the life of a single man who lives its truth out
before us.

Finally, we shall speak of one more side from
which men dispute the significance of Jesus for this
age. They ask, Why set so much store by personality? After all, ideas only, they say, possess significance in history. Not only men, but also
thoughts, are realities. Thoughts are even the
supremely true realities. Whatever is personal is
accidental; spiritual thought is the necessary and
important element. Men are vessels, it is true,
of the Spirit, but the Spirit alone is the cus-
todian of truth, and the development of the Spirit
alone has value. Lift up your thoughts, they say, to
the idea of Christ and cast off this bondage to the
historic Jesus!

But no idea of Christ, however ideal, would ever
have been able to give us what the living Jesus has
given us. If the matter of chief moment were the
development of ideas, then the ideas of Christ might
take the place of the living Jesus. Our chief concern, however, is not over the development of ideas,
but over the salvation of man, over the renewal of
life, over the re-making of the world. For these
ends, the rich, warm influence of fresh phases of

reality in manifestation through a human life
needed. The divinest event in the history of th
world, the greatest, happiest, and most significan
experience destined for us is just this, that luminous divinity is streaming forth upon us from a
human life, not with the cold radiance of an idea,
but as a heart-warming light sent out from and
reflected in the character of a human being. To let
the living Jesus become desiccated into an idea im-
poverishes us just as much as does the failure to
penetrate through the living Jesus to the mind of
God which is the source of His illumination. The
one oversight casts a chill over the history of the
world, the other fills it with gloom.

What, then, is the special significance of Jesus for
the present age? Or, to put the question more defi-
nitely, Who are the people for whom Jesus possesses
significance to-day? The whole preceding discussion supplies the answer. Jesus can be of service to
all those who seek to attain a true humanity. This
seeking and yearning is, as yet, not really strongly
prevalent in the world. Very few people have the
faintest notion yet of the splendor and nobility of
true humanity. In spite of our high industrial
development, the culture of man's inner nature is
still dominated by a barbarism which greatly alarms
those with the insight to appraise it correctly. But
the signs of coming change increase in number.

Nietzsche exercised a far-reaching, beneficial influence in spite of the childish interpretation put upon
his suggestions by many people who would have us
believe that his pose of the superman, his tragic

titude to the world, his critique of morality, and
s hostility to Christianity exhaust the man. But
t least he taught us to pronounce the word man
with new reverence again. Nietzsche's best was his
insatiable longing. That he has set before men a
new ideal of man above that of Christianity is certainly and obviously untrue. By pronouncing egoism to be more sacred than love, pugnacity than
peaceableness, raillery than seriousness, he hoped to
surpass and to destroy Christianity.

How we ought to regard this particular effort of
Nietzsche is no longer a matter of dispute. Jesus
as we have become acquainted with Him, in spite
of all His majestic seriousness, lived in regions of
joy which make everything that Nietzsche has said
about happiness appear hollow and false. In saying: "I thank thee, O Father; Lord of heaven and
earth, because thou hast hid these things from the
wise and prudent, and hast revealed them unto
babes. Even so, Father; for so it seemed good in
thy sight," Jesus gave in these unpretentious words
a more genuine and impressive utterance to joy than
can be found in all the poets of the world. We were
deeply moved by the glimmer of heavenly joy which
rests upon many a parable of Jesus in our previous
study of them. Such is the species of joy animating
the very man whose seriousness often almost over-
whelms with its force. "But I say unto you, That
every idle word that men shall speak, they shall give
account thereof in the day of judgment." "But I
say unto you, That whosoever is angry with his
brother without a cause shall be in danger of the

judgment." Never has any one imparted to spee
a sense of greater weight, nor to an inner feeling
sense of greater importance than Jesus has don
here.

So Jesus was by no means a tame man who desired
ease and peace and feared struggle. He was not the
man described by Nietzsche. The call to combat
which we hear ringing ever more and more clearly
in His words is so exalted in tone that in the presence of its challenge all the striving in our lives seems
no more than sluggish inactivity. "Think not that
I am come to send peace on earth: I came not to
send peace, but a sword: For I am come to set a
man at variance against his father, and the daughter
against her mother. . . . And a man's foes shall be
they of his own household." "If any man come to
me, and hate not his father, and mother,—yea, and
his own life, also, he cannot be my disciple." But
we must put this call to combat with the unconquerable trust which, as we have seen, Jesus had in God,
as a towering fortress of peace in the midst of all
elements of struggle, and take the two together:
"For not a hair falls from your head without the
Father's will." And although Nietzsche wished to
give egoism precedence over love, neither he, nor
anyone else, has ever conceived of so sacred an egoism as did Jesus in his saying: "Be ye therefore
perfect, even as your Father which is in heaven is
perfect." "But seek ye first the kingdom of God,
and His righteousness, and all these things shall be
added unto you." "And if thy right eye offend thee,
pluck it out, and cast it from thee!" "For what is a

an profited, if he shall gain the whole world, and ose his own soul?" On the spiritual heights on which Jesus lived, egoism and love blend into an eternal unity. For love is, as we have learned, nothing other than life serving as a conduit for the life of God, the highest kind of life possible to man.

Anyone who wishes to understand the whole difference between Nietzsche and Jesus needs only learn to sense how narrow and forced Nietzsche's egoism is in spite of its ambitious aim. Nietzsche wishes always to differentiate himself from others and to triumph over them. Let this attitude be compared with the lofty, untrammeled self-assertion and unlimited self-devotion of Jesus, and the opposition of Nietzsche to Jesus can be regarded only as the result of misunderstanding, and his proclamation of a higher ideal of man only as illusion. Indeed, when we learn, as Jesus learned, how to unite with perfect naturalness the highest zeal and the highest joy in life, vigorous combat and a deep sense of freedom from the necessity of combat, untrammeled self-assertion and self-chosen devotion— we shall then be men!

But the secret of Jesus' sway over mankind still eludes our attempts to expose it. Perhaps we may come to perceive more clearly the real nature of the humanity that shines forth for us in Jesus if we turn our gaze for a moment away from Him to ourselves. We men of this present age permit ourselves to expend our whole strength on external things. The life outside us draws us incessantly away from the life within us. The abundance of events that

stream by us, calling to us sometimes to do an
sometimes to bear suffering, lures us out of our
selves. Once one of us begins to live on his own
soul's resources he becomes aware, frightfully aware,
how completely he has been living only for outward,
alien things. Our life is a ceaseless round of strain
and diversion in eternal alteration. Our serious
occupations are all with the external, and there we
seek, also, our recreations. Men to-day are able to
leave home and do astonishingly much, but they are
not able to live upon their inner resources. When
Thoreau tells us, "Happy is he who can always find
joy in his own thoughts!" his caution awakens in
us to-day hardly a pang of uneasiness and longing.
The wealth and variety of the things we know and
can do is out of all proportion to the poverty of
spirit that stares us in the face when we are left
alone. We have all gone astray and lost our way
in things material—the scholar in his investigations,
the politician in his campaigns, the merchant in his
business. The challenge to which our age has re-
sponded is the conquest of the outer world; this is
its badge of destruction, and it is its misfortune as
well.

The task to which this present age should respond
now is to turn its gaze toward Jesus from the pit
which it has dug. A mysteriously powerful inwardness will soon begin to light up and shine in our life.
All the many-sided appeals of the outer world cannot prevail against the pleas of this inner world;
rather is this outer world magnificently set ablaze
by the light of this inner world which eclipses its

wn sun. Anyone of His parables, for example, the
homely narrative of the Sower, so wonderfully transfigured by the insight of Jesus, is illustration and
proof enough of the way in which the world outside
Him was set ablaze by the light that burned within
Him. As purely and as calmly as the reflection
which the world cast into the soul of Jesus, so joy-
fully and richly did it glimmer in the light cast upon
it from the flaming core of His being.

It is a newly clothed world which stands before
us in the splendor of spiritual insight contained in
the sayings of Jesus. The high privilege of manhood is there set forth: we are called to create the
world anew. With energy secured from the luminous center of our being we may, indeed we must,
renew the world in which we live. It is true, as
Tolstoi said, that God creates a new world for every
fresh man born. It is not less true that every man
may offer a new world of his own making to God.
And the world which a man shapes out of his experiences, to which he gives birth anew, is his individual own and remains forever unique. Thus, the
evolution of the world waits for man to coöperate
in order to continue its further advance in him.
After this incomplete evolution has once crossed
over into the spiritual, the world during every
moment in which it is born anew out of the inner
life of a man is re-fashioned and perfected as if by
miracle. Nowhere do we perceive these deep secrets
of human nature more vividly than when we fix our
gaze upon the surcharged inward life of Jesus.

This opens up the way, also, for us to obtain an

insight into another defect of our time. Daily exis
ence is split up into many diverse fragments to a.
extent unknown in any former age. We have learneo
only too well to set our life at variance by dividing
our attention between duty and inclination, profes-
sion and family, the ideal and the real, faith and
knowledge, religion and life—and who knows how
many diversities more? Two souls, or rather many
souls, dwell in every breast. There is no one among
us who does not suffer, consciously or unconsciously,
from a dismembered and disrupted state of his nature. The man of the present day is an aggregate
of the things that he knows and can do, held together
by a mechanical bond, like fagots in bundles, and
not a growth from a common root like the twigs of
a tree.

In spite of all the impression of abundance which
His life makes upon us, we become acquainted in
Jesus with what unity is, with the inner, organic
unity of a full-orbed human being. It is not the
intensive, though benumbed, concentration of the
holy men of India, but it is a unity of the highest
activities of life in combination, which renews itself
through a continual process of change. Instead of
calling this quality unity in Jesus, we could describe
it also as genuineness, an elemental genuineness
present in every utterance of His life. How different the behavior of Jesus seems in the Court of the
Temple from His bearing in the Garden of Gethsemane, and yet how impressively the same exalted
sincerity is exhibited on both occasions. How unlike
the expression in His eyes as they rested upon the

inful was the fire in them which flashed out against
His enemies, and yet how indubitably do we know
in both instances that it is the same face. Whatever
knock might rap upon the soul of Jesus, it always
gave out the one same tone. However manifold
those sounds they always chord, and no false tone
occurs among them. The key in which His spirit
was pitched is unmistakable. We seem able to distinguish it yet to-day, such life is there in it; and it
makes us feel that we are going to hear it eternally,
so unfathomable is it. Or, to use modern speech, we
find in Jesus a life that has genuine unity, which
always speaks and acts in character, although it was
a life of most intensive vitality. Back of the nature
that Jesus reveals to us no other nature lies concealed; His innermost nature lives itself out into the
open in everything, unhindered and unrestrained.
Everything in Him sprang to meet any demand of
the moment, and thus everything He said and did
became a revelation of the depth of His soul. A
transparent, luminous genuineness which is a source
of noble refreshment to our souls—this describes
best the impression which we receive from the nature
of Jesus.

Let us look once more closely at our own age.
Have we not become bondmen of the world? Our
life is carried on under a continual pressure and
stress, even that life at its best. Hour after hour
without end some duty imperatively commands us.
One duty hands us over to the next unto the end
of life, just as "a waterpail is passed from hand to
hand" down a whole line of men who are fighting a

fire. It is not we who do our duty, but duty after
duty uses us to get itself performed. We are the
instruments of the world's will, it is true, but not
conscious and voluntary instruments. We are har-
nessed to the world's chariot and draw it, one man
pulling better, another worse, some straining eagerly
at the traces, and others grudging every step of the
way—this is the whole difference. And he who gets
a chance to take the harness off puts it back on, for
otherwise he would not know how to pass the time.

In sharpest contrast, how great is the freedom and
sovereignty with which Jesus stands at the throttle
of His life! His life appears to be something which
by an act of the highest freedom He is weaving into
the world's life. Nothing that He does is wrung
reluctantly from Him, everything carries the seal
of a royal voluntariness. Jesus is Lord even over
His destined death; He confiscates it and makes it
an act of His own will. "No one taketh my life from
me, but I lay it down of myself." Events crowd
upon Him with power in them to slay, but when
His life goes forth from Him it is He that is giving,
and not they that are taking, a voluntary outcome
of a purpose of His own. Even in hours of deepest
misery His life chants a high song of freedom, the
like of which no poet has ever created. We wonder
over and over again as we look at Him to what glorious and noble a freedom man, that particle of the
cosmos, can raise himself. The words of the poet,
"Man was created free and thus shall he ever
remain," take on a wholly new significance after we
have penetrated into the life of Jesus.

But even these thoughts on life are only presentiments concerning man's true humanity. Its secret cannot be dissected by thought, but waits to be revealed to us in the process of creative experimental living. We will put only one more query, Whence came this true humanity to Jesus? Our inquiry is not about the birth of His body, but about the birth of His soul. And the answer is clear: this true humanity did not painfully develop itself out of the depths of man, but was born of the resources of God. Jesus never sought to track the true capacities of humanity to their ultimate hiding place; He desired the uttermost of God. His chief thought was not how to develop the splendid possibilities of human nature, but how to carry devotion to the will of God ever one step further. The glimpses we possess of the life Jesus lived in the inward depths of His own nature, its fundamental genuineness and elemental freedom, are, indeed, views of an unspeakable beauty. That life, however, was "added unto Him"; the life into which He put all His mind and heart and strength was His life of devotion to the will of God. He lives thus on initiatives from within and not compulsions from without, because His surrender of Himself to God is so complete; His life is sincerity itself, because He belongs so decisively to God; He lives so free of interference from men, because He serves God so willingly. This is the process of gestation that led up to the birth of the Son of God. His birth divine is not a single event occurring in a few moments, but He is born anew during every moment of His acceptance of His life

as a gift from God. The secret of true humani
cannot be fathomed any deeper by us. The mor
completely a man carries his devotion to God, the
more gloriously does he enter upon his true humanity. Released from all the illusions of subjectivism
and all the tangents of individualism, the life of man
thus attains the full stature of its true greatness.
The divine necessity laid upon our life is the crown
of its human glory. Out of the depths of the cosmos God comes and invades our life and sweeps it
thus onto the heights. Every other kind of existence gets shown up finally to be hollow and unstable,
to be caricature and disintegration, to be deception
and illusion. Assuredly we owe nothing we possess to ourselves; not our nature, for that is a gift;
not our will, which is also part of that gift of
nature. Just as certainly, therefore, only innermost
union with divine purpose at work in the world will
draw us out of ourselves into our true life, our genuine humanity. No poet and no thinker will ever
perform the miracle required to invent a higher form
of humanity. But how beautifully does the divine
when allowed shine through the fleshly envelope of
a human being! How distinctly does the divine
speak even in the weak language of a human life
that offers to be its vehicle.

But how can we keep on talking as we have all
along so confidently of God, as if no exceptions at
all would be taken, and as if it were not the gravest
question that encounters us just here? For has
not the most vehement dispute of the present age
broken out over the question whether we are war-

nted in speaking at all about God? Has Nietzsche
ot issued the weighty fiat: God is dead, dead for
all time? And has his dictum not been greeted with
enthusiasm by hundreds as a charter of deliverance
from the old and as a watchword for the new? This
was how it was received at the time, and is still.
But few people know that Nietzsche, nevertheless,
himself concealed a doubting heart behind his con-
fident exterior, and that in the most unperturbed
hours of his life at its close he could write: "What
you call the self-disintegration of God is only His
rejuvenation. ... You shall soon see Him enthroned
again beyond the reach of your thoughts of good
and evil!" But few people have followed this phase
of Nietzsche's thought. Our own conviction is, however, that in the present struggle about what to
think of God, Jesus will also, more than all else,
help us to make up our minds. Jesus is of the
utmost significance, therefore, not only to those who
seek contact with the true humanity, but also for
those who seek contact with God. Into the exter-
nalities of belief in God we cannot and need not
enter here.

If God is, He stands high above any conception of
Him that ever dwelt in the souls of men. But there
are questions which stand out with prominence.
One is, Whence is the world? We are not asking
whether it was made at some one moment of time,
or has always existed; but we do ask whether it is
grounded in a source into which human reason can
have an insight, whether this background is an
empty nothing or is Spirit, a living Spirit who has

thought out and still thinks out this world, who hold
and bears this world up by the force of His own
Being. Likewise we must ask, What kind of government rules in the world?   Our inquiry is not
whether eternal, inexorable laws dominate, or the
despotism of a personal will, but we do ask, Does
unreason or reason preside over the events of the
world? Are the laws and the events of nature only
soulless equations of elements back of which our
means of inquiry cannot penetrate, or does Spirit
manifest itself in all being, and is Spirit active in
all events? Lastly, still another question is to be
faced, In what direction does the world tend? We
ask not whether the world will end in a sudden
catastrophe, or whether it will continue to develop
higher forms of life, but we do ask, Who sets the
world its aim, its purpose, and its future? Is it left
to man to define the significance which the world
shall have, or does that rest with a higher power
which knows well what it plans, which can be sought
out by men and is willing to be found by men, a
power which strives to realize its aim in and through
coöperation with us? We seek to gain an answer
to these questions from the soul of the present day,
inadequately though they may be stated and apt as
they are to be misunderstood, since human language
can speak only thus imperfectly upon the highest
problems. We understand that these highest questions may appear to many to-day to be superfluous
and obsolete; yet they recur and stir the human
spirit again and again, ever wearing an aspect more
searching.

What, then, does Jesus mean to us, as we face this problem of God? Shall we think of Him as one who belongs to a vanished past? Or as one who lived in an entirely different network of human relations and with people employing different conceptions from our own? Can we know Him, indeed, only through intermediaries? Let us consider our answer well. The unseen power which became visible in Jesus on the plane of our world-history proved itself truly superior to the world and victorious over it. In spite of all obstacles, this power went irresistibly on its way to victory. Nothing was able to overpower it; everything bowed in submission to it. With their whole strength His opponents strove in His lifetime against this power which was in Jesus, and when all was over they had not accomplished their own ends, but even against their own will it was the aims of this power they had fulfilled! Never does awe so strongly overpower us and exalt our feelings as when the veils which conceal from our eyes the purpose of the world's will seem to be torn apart, and for a moment we can take a look into the depths of the mystery and peer at the Spirit of the world where He sits in deep tranquillity before the loom of Time, interweaving the thousands of strands that make up the pattern of the universe. One look sanctifies us for all time. Blind law, evil, disaster, and everything else that has been made to serve again and again as a contradiction of the fact of divine power are exhibited here as acknowledging the superiority of this power; all these forces combined, it is made clear, cannot circumvent this power, but must aid in the completion of its ends.

And not only in Jesus' lifetime, but also in our time may we see how this power goes on its way to victory, unconfused and unconquerable, as it forges for itself out of the most refractory elements weapons of victory for the conquest of the world. Where the spirit of Jesus becomes alive, evil loses its power to blast and is able only to bless; there it becomes powerless to hinder and is compelled to help toward the victory. Where the spirit of Jesus becomes alive, the laws of nature give up their rigidness and by putting themselves at the service of a spirit working in our behalf lose their power to hinder and turn into helpers, just as distress and death were compelled once for Jesus to become a help. Is it not here, then, that we stand face to face with the power which governs and guides the world? How wonderfully welcome this very idea is to us to-day, who so often feel as if we were helplessly entangled in the inexorable meshes of natural law, and almost forced to believe that we must surrender in despair to nature's despotic rule. Now it is as if something spiritual inhabiting the background of the world spoke to us through all events and circumstances, thus: It is I, who rules all! It is I, who am conqueror over all!

Is it possible to feel that there is yet more to be learned concerning this power? Yes; for through Jesus this power takes root among men as a mighty and a truly majestic force at work for our salvation, while this will works its way into the race through

the best human thinking, choice human feeling, and
choice human willing as its channels, yet its will
for the redemption of the world, more than human
in nature and might, towers far above the plane
of our mortal life, and with a voice as of a spirit
invites us to become its children. We stand not
face to face with a rigid power when we look through
the eyes of Jesus into the mystery of our existence,
but with a living soul which makes itself known
that we may have fellowship with it, spirit like unto
our spirit that desires with all the force of its powerful will the salvation of the world. To men accus-
tomed like ourselves to see everywhere nothing but
natural forces at work, how great is the relief
afforded by faint insight into the significance which
the Spirit gives to the events of Time!

Is it possible to feel that there is even yet more to
learn concerning this power? In casting about for
an answer, let us look at Jesus once more. His
active, human nature with all its vitality and vivid-
ness of feeling seems to disappear from our sight as
we track it toward its center, and to become lost to
us by coalescence, as it were, with the light of the
Spirit at its purest intensity. This experience also
makes it clear that the essence of that light became
visible in our world by becoming embodied in a
human being pervaded through and through with
its vital power. This light at its purest intensity—
but why try to lay hold of the indescribable with
words? So also when we have spoken of "a holy
kindness" as the disposition of the central energy
of the universe. How dull this phrase sounds in

comparison with the strong and tender disposition toward his fellows which dwelt in Jesus, which guided His will with luminous purity and tinctured His feelings with unalloyed benevolence! As within the solid, hard crystal gleams the distant, intangible sun, something is aglow in Jesus that is of the earth and is yet above the earth, and this and nothing else is responsible for the victory of Jesus over the darkness of the world. If this spiritual energy is now capable of overcoming all opposition, may it not then also be the power that in the very beginning thought and willed the world and all that is therein into being? And here again, how this point of view comforts and assures those of us who had begun to feel ourselves to be only children of nature, sprung from the womb of the accidental, and destined to sink into the grave of futility! And does not this Spirit, this loving Spirit of the world, summon us to assist in the completion of His plans and purposes?

But proof, proof! is the cry of the age. All this is words; where are the proofs? We make no secret of the fact that there is no proof possible. Nor shall we try to keep it a secret that any proof that could be offered would be unworthy. Proof is by nature a compulsion; and nowhere is compulsion more out of place than where the call is for us to rise up and lay hold of something. We stand as free agents in the presence of the world's secret. We stand as free agents, also, in the presence of that marvelous life through which the secret of the world reveals itself to us in Jesus. Is it true that contact with Jesus brings us nearest to the eternal truth? No man can answer that question for another, and no angel will answer it for him. No proof will be found to assure us, nor any authority to authenticate this truth for us. Freely must we decide each for himself whether his conscience, his world, his nature grants him authority to answer, Yes! This responsibility is our patent of nobility. Our decision ought to be sincere and unaffected by any of our sympathies and antipathies. Our decision ought to be of the nature of a recognition, as of a father by his son, or of a congenial spirit by a kindred nature. None of us, however, will achieve a full assurance until the Father has introduced him as a son into the innermost community of Spirit—until God has begun to dwell in him. Only what is part and parcel of ourselves is unassailable by any uncertainty. The more our life coalesces with the nature of God, the more we shall surpass ourselves in certainty, the more we shall experience how evil and sin dissolve into victory and blessing. We shall thus grow into a state of development which exceeds nature and the achievements of all cultures, one that shall usher in the dawn of a new world.

But what will become of the old Christianity with all the oppressive weight of its great dogmas of the Trinity, Atonement, Redemption, Regeneration? After its two thousand years of history that still speak so potently, shall a new Christianity supersede it, and shall this be produced in an age which for religious genius can not at all be compared with the past? Is it any wonder that the champions of the old faith reject the idea as a base parting with our heritage? On the other hand, those who stake all their hopes on the future regard the suggestion as a caricature. Both agree that Christianity shall remain as it ever has been and that it must be accepted or rejected in that form. Let us not put the new wine into old wine-skins which the vigor of this new wine will burst; neither let us put the old wine into new wine-skins which will spoil its taste.

But on what ground, we answer, is the present age to be denied the privilege of giving an expression of its own to its experience of Jesus? Was the experience of Jesus that fell to the lot of St. Francis truly the same kind of experience in all points as that which befell Luther, or Schleiermacher? Does not Jesus belong as much to men living to-day as to men in the past? Is it not our plain right, even our urgent duty, to substitute for every mediation through history a face-to-face approach? Whether or not the outcome be a continued espousal of Christianity, we seek truth, the kind of truth that can be called our own. We seek what truth there is for us in Jesus, even in Him only what presents itself as the truth which our personal experience of life confirms. If Jesus is indeed really greater than His followers, if He really surpasses our human statements and dogmas concerning Him, then He has not hitherto been known and understood to the limit of His being, and it is possible for a new age to add to the sum of human understanding of Him. Our experience of Jesus may be incomplete, but that experience is the ore from which our truth, our joy, our exaltation, and our edification must be extracted.

Now however, in the backward look from the post of observation supplied by our experience of Jesus into the world of the traditional Christian dogmas, that world begins to renew its life before our eyes and exert on us something of its old attraction. Is it not still really true that the yearning of God for men was present in Jesus, and that in seeking after men He fairly impersonated Him? Is it not still true that the divine will required of Him His suffering, that where two wills were so one in temper both may fairly be said to have borne that suffering? Does not the word sacrifice still really express the content of His life to its depths? Can it well be denied that He lived this life of sacrifice wholly and entirely in our behalf? Was He not in the greatness of His heart really far more troubled by the sins of men than they were themselves, and ever so much more concerned in the removal of the load of sin from men? Is it not still true that the object lesson of His life and death is able, as can be said of no other life, to release men from the isolation of their old world of egoism, to unite them by a bond of spirit most inwardly to God, to awaken them and to make them over into new beings? That God came to the earth, suffered and died and redeemed the world through His death, is the way the old dogmas were proclaimed to mankind. Are we not prepared now to perceive the truth countersigned by our own experience shining with a living light through these hard statements? Do we not now feel all at once as if our voice, which so recently we believed would have to sing its pean of faith all alone, chimes in harmony with the voices of the Christian centuries that preceded us? Does it not move us deeply to perceive how marvelously Christianity has always been able to renew itself, ever extracting new increments of blessing from within Jesus and from its own interior being.

This must not mean, be it emphasized, that differences between the two interpretations shall be minimized by ambiguities of statement. We do not any longer, as men did once, run a sharp line of cleavage between the death of Jesus and His life, but we see the meaning of His death in His life, the meaning of His life in His death. We do not try any longer to determine the exact limits between the divine in Jesus and the human in Him, but would rather put it that an elemental kinship exists between the human and the divine, and therefore look upon the incarnation of God in man as involving a process more natural, more inward, and more vital. We do not any longer try to drive a wedge between the humanity of Jesus and the humanity of the rest of mankind, but prefer to credit Jesus with a nobility set for us as our goal; so we feel just as deeply that He belongs to us as we feel that He is superior to us. We speak no longer the language of dualistic metaphysics, but use the language of modern psychology; for the forms of thought that belonged to the ancient cultus of sacrifice, we substitute the forms of thought in use in the ethics of to-day. The object lesson in salvation which occurred once in history is to us an example of eternal laws of salvation that are universally valid wherever the divine struggles with that which is lower than itself. God shall become man also in us; in us, too, God wills to bear suffering for the good of men, and also in us God must complete His work of eternal redemption. It is amazing to observe how all this celestial content, now in its weak beginnings within us, was in Jesus the fundamental content of His life.

In this way the old dogmas yield to us a ravishing residuum of lofty spiritual significance. And there has been no intention whatever in what has just been said to galvanize dead dogmas into the appearance of life, but a simple purpose to express the plain truth as we have come to know it and feel it.

Much in the world of ideas has changed since the time of our forefathers; God and the world stand no longer over against each other in such sharp antithesis; the world and God of course are not one and the same for us, but God is alive from our point of view in the world, the world alive in God. Historically speaking, we have incorporated Spinoza into our thinking. Metaphysical questions find us more critically inclined than hitherto; instead of the confidence which proceeds from dogmatizing has come the caution which thinking yields. The limits of the human mind have become evident and unmistakable, which means that we have sat at the feet of Kant. The realm of the soul has undergone refinement in manifold ways as our spiritual faculties have developed a greater degree of susceptibility. To think of two Natures coexisting in one and the same Person has become intellectually impossible

for us. We are committed to-day to a livelier per
ception of human worth, for great poets and writers
have not celebrated the soul of mankind in vain.
To mention only one, we have incorporated Goethe
into our thinking. Nature around us has become
likewise more familiar; incomparably clearer is our
insight into the ruling forces of the physical world-
order; the law of causation and the concept of development have profoundly influenced the modern
mind, which means that we have incorporated New-
ton and Darwin into our thinking. Our old earth is
no longer the sole stage of universal history. Our
intellectual horizon extends to the limits of the visible universe, which means that we have incorporated Copernicus and Kepler into our thinking.
Changes, indeed, which are staggeringly immense!

And now to sum up: What has been the effect of
these immense changes upon our attitude to Jesus?
We reply that in spite of these extraordinary revolu-
tions in our intellectual world Jesus still captivates
the human race with the splendor of the divine that
radiates from Him. His image has become brighter
and more vivid—that is all. Still He waits with a
welcome all His own for those who seek God, waits
for those who seek the true humanity. A discovery
without parallel is in store for him who, in some
hour of calm, penetrates all the theories of the centuries and comes out face to face with the human
glory of Jesus. This Man once did live here! This
Man once did walk our earth! There is a thought
with substance enough to grip us our whole life
long.

But none the less overwhelming is the reaction accompanying that other discovery that God was in Jesus. In Him we behold God living right down among us, powerfully active in our behalf; God as He is willing also to live in us, and bear, and struggle, and conquer. Here is the life of God, clothing itself in a human form; and conversely, a unit of human nature transfigured by the presence of God.

Nothing isolated and nothing absolutely different does Jesus longer need to be for us. He was born with unique endowments, to be sure, and He lived under conditions which cannot be reproduced, but if we seek to go beyond these facts we get lost in the depths of the divine mystery of life. As our Master and Leader, however, He seeks our company, too, not in order to discourage us by His superiority, but to raise us above ourselves through our participation in His spirit. Jesus lives for men; for this reason only do men live for Jesus. Freely and royally we may take from Him what we can and receive from Him yet to-day, as we can obtain them from no other source—renewal of life for ourselves, fulfillment of our ideals for our world, and ultimate union with God.

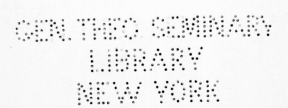